Pu

Enete]

6504 N Omaha Ave

Oklahoma City, OK 73116 (USA)

1st publication of

Becoming an Expat: Mexico

Steinberg-Di Stefano, Noah
Enete, Shannon

Becoming an Expat: Mexico / Noah Steinberg-Di Stefano,
Shannon Enete

ISBN-13: 978-1-938216-14-5

ISBN-10: 1938216148

Printed in the United States of America

www.EneteEnterprises.com

DEDICATION

To my parents, James and Paola, for keeping me cultured and always encouraging me to take risks and get beautifully lost along the way. I love you.

~ Noah

Table Of Contents:

«INTRODUCTION»

Mexico may be the most stereotyped country on earth. Known around the world for scandalous spring-break beaches and gun slinging drug lords, the country is often overlooked for its amazingly diverse cultural landscape. You have to wade through these stereotypes to discover the rich culture rooted in Mexico that makes it one of the top destinations in the world for travelers and expats alike. If there's one thing that I have learned since moving here, it's this is a country full of surprises. From the Aztec pyramids of Palenque and the vast agave fields of Jalisco, to the dizzying chaotic pulse of the Distrito Federal, each of Mexico's 31 states has something unique to offer.

If you're a culture junkie like me, you will notice Mexico's infectious ex-factor. It's something that is hard to pinpoint, but makes you feel alive. Maybe it's the Mariachi's serenading a group of diners in the plaza, the colorful colonial architecture and cobblestone streets, or the gregarious eating and drinking culture that delves much deeper than tacos and Coronas. Maybe it's the Mexican people, always eager to open their doors to visitors and show them what their country and Latin hospitality is all about.

While reading this no-nonsense guide, I encourage you to cast your preconceptions aside. I'm not going to tell you that Mexico is a carefree paradise, nor will I try to convince you that anything you've ever heard about Mexico is a lie. I am here to set the record straight by sharing with you the best and the worst the country has to offer without an ulterior motive. We are not selling a dream, a house, a service, or a lifestyle, just a guide to help you decide for yourself if Mexico is right for you, and if so, what the hell to do about it!

«THE BASICS»

History

Mexico's history is tumultuous to say the least. Like other Latin American countries, its colonial past has created a present day society rife with divisions and inequality. It's important to understand some basics of Mexican history in order to fully grasp the current political and societal situations. We'll make it as painless as possible.

Before the Spanish arrived, Mexico was populated by a variety of indigenous groups, all with their own set of cultural traditions and social systems. When Cortes arrived in the Port of Veracruz in 1519, he took advantage of the high tensions between tribes by waging war with the Aztecs and recruiting rival tribes to topple the empire. There are numerous books devoted to this subject alone, but this isn't one of them.

What proceeded was essentially 300 years of enslavement and exploitation of the indigenous people and their land. The Spanish expropriated the indigenous land and redistributed it amongst themselves. They tore the land apart in search of precious minerals, like silver and gold. Silver mines in regions like Guanajuato brought immense wealth to the region in the 16th century. At the time, Mexico was the world's number one source of precious metals. The Spanish conquistadors all but stripped the country clean of its minerals, thus establishing a culture of dependence and exploitation that continues to plague Mexico today.

Independence

By the early 1800's, the people of Mexico had enough. They joined together to fight for their freedom from Spain. On September 16th, 1810 (now celebrated as Mexico's independence day), legend has it that in the town Dolores Hidalgo, the priest Miguel Hidalgo rang his church bells and cried out to the local indigenous people, calling on them to rebel against the Spaniards and reclaim the land that was stolen from their forefathers. This revolt is seen as a turning point in the fight for independence. Miguel Hidalgo and his army marched on Mexico City in 1811 and almost seized the capital, but were defeated in the Battle of Calderon Bridge. Miguel Hidalgo was captured and hung, thus he became a famous martyr for the cause. His death would inspire successors to keep fighting on the path of liberation.

After three centuries of Spanish rule and oppression, Mexico finally won its independence in September of 1821. When the excitement of freedom and independence wore off, Mexicans came to the realization that they had a country to rebuild. As you can imagine, the transition to a stable, functioning democracy was not without its pitfalls.

The challenge for Mexico was not unique. There were many countries undergoing a similarly tumultuous divorce from Spanish rule. They all needed to build an infrastructure and democracy from the ground up.

Porifio Diaz & The Mexican Revolution (1910-1940)

Porifio Diaz ruled Mexico with an iron fist for 35 years, from 1876-1911. On the positive side, his dictatorship is marked by a major spike in foreign investment from Europe and the United States which lead to modernization and growth of the Mexican economy. That would have been great had the riches ever trickled down to the hands of the people. Only a minuscule percentage of the population benefited from these reforms while the majority of Mexicans toiled in virtual slavery, serving the interests of the rich.

The Mexican revolution was a direct response to widening inequality across the nation and lack of freedom of speech. As Diaz's grasp of power began to loosen, a group of Mexican exiles organized a well-coordinated coup from outposts in the United States.

Zapatista Movement

On January 1st, 1994, thousands of armed indigenous farmers descended from their homes in the highlands of Chiapas to the City of San

Cristobal de las Casas and declared autonomy from the Mexican state. They were fed up from decades of neglect and discrimination in their own land. They were done with isolation of their children from schools and their women from hospitals. Their modest demands included land ownership rights, dignity, education, and the right to decide their own future. They called themselves Zapatistas in honor of Emiliano Zapata, one of the heroes of the Mexican Revolution who was a champion for equality and indigenous rights.

After years of beating their heads against the wall trying to create change through the democratic process, the Zapatistas realized they needed to change their approach. They took up arms because they had no voice or power to direct their destiny. There were a number of bloody battles between the Zapatistas and the Mexican army, as well as

unprovoked massacres committed by the military. The oppression of the indigenous people continues to persist.

In 2003, after years of struggle, the Zapatistas shifted away from armed conflict and towards autonomous communities. Throughout the states of Chiapas and Oaxaca, you will find signs marking autonomous Zapatistas territories. If you ever have

EXPAT EXPERIENCE

Mexico gets a very bad rap in the States. Most areas are extremely safe

and the Mexican people are wonderful! The culture is wonderful. Families are much tighter. There is no assisted living— children take care of their older parent and grandparents when the need arises. Medical care is much less expensive than in the U.S. and generally much more caring and surprisingly, frequently better quality with state of the art equipment.

~ Gerald Rapp, 70 year old expat from New York City

the opportunity to visit one of these communities, do it!

Crime

Time to address the elephant in the room. I think the number one question I heard when I decided to move to Mexico was, "Is it safe?" In the United States, our news is polluted by tidbits from drug cartel violence. You are only shown one side of the coin. In fact, I would argue you don't even see an entire side! So I'm going to tell it like it is.

Do you have to take certain precautions when living and traveling in Mexico? Absolutely. I take the same precautions I would in any other major city such as: New York, Chicago, New Orleans, Washington D.C., etc. You need to research the regions in Mexico that you are considering moving to just as you would in Canada or the US. You wouldn't move to south-central Los Angeles without reading about the crime would you? The same goes for Mexico.

The violent crime in Mexico is concentrated along drug and human trafficking routes along the U.S.-Mexican Border. Cities like Nuevo Laredo, Ciudad Juarez, and Chihuahua in the north are battlegrounds for drug cartels fighting for territory. They aren't enticing weekend getaway destinations. Acapulco, once one of Mexico's most popular tourist destination, has even seen a surge in violent crime in recent years, presumably due to the redirection of lucrative drug trafficking routes from Central America and the Caribbean.   Again, it's important to stress that any violence is almost exclusively between drug cartels and is concentrated in the residential areas a safe distance from Acapulco's beaches and business district. We are not seeing foreigners picked up off the streets. If you don't plan on working or interacting with the drug cartel, then I don't foresee a problem. I've had a lovely time in Acapulco. Just like a visit to New York City doesn't mean you will have to rub elbows with the Italian mafia.

Economic inequality in Mexico is always in your face. Because of this, robbery and petty theft are fairly common. Like anywhere, how safe you feel is dependent on your street smarts. I'm going to give you a few safety tips to put your mind at ease.

Crime is a touchy topic no matter what country or city is being scrutinized. If you are the type of person that is uneasy with any sort of unrest, then you have many regions of Mexico to avoid. However, speaking as someone who has lived in Mexico and traveled extensively, it is certainly not as dangerous as international news proclaims. Many people make assumptions about safety in Mexico because the only news they are seeing is negative. You'll see a report of the climbing murder rate in Ciudad Juarez or gruesome kidnappings along the border. I must stress that Mexico is a very big country. The 15th largest country in the world, in fact. If I told you that there was a major outbreak of gang violence in North Carolina, would you cancel your trip to Florida? New Orleans and Chicago are both cities with violent crime rates higher than most cities in Mexico. Does that mean you would decline an invitation to Mardi Gras or refuse to go to a Chicago Cubs game? Probably not. As a general rule, if you stay sharp, know where you're going, and mind your own business, you'll be safe and sound in Mexico.

EXPAT EXPERIENCE

"I feel safer in Mexico than I did when I lived in Dayton, Ohio. My home was robbed when I was sleeping in Ohio and I often think about how lucky I was that I didn't wake up. I can walk down the street at night in Coatepec and I feel very safe."

~ Susan Mills, expat from Dayton, Ohio

SEX & Public Displays of Affection (P.D.A.)

In almost every public park, metro station, or bus stop, you are bound to see starry-eyed lovers locked in a deep make-out session. It might be because most Mexicans live with their families until they get married, so there isn't always a 'room to get'. The sex-scene in Mexico is oddly connected to the tightly-knit family dynamic. Let me explain. You've got the majority of single men and woman, often very successful and perfectly capable of going out on their own, living with their families well into their 30's. Mexican women, for example, seem to have their conscience plugged in to their mothers intuition that tells them they should be looking for a husband, not a lover. A Mexican woman might hook up with you, but will almost certainly pause in the middle to let you know she's never done this before, or Dios Mio, what would her mother say!

MUSIC & DANCE

It's fitting that a section on music and dance is preceded by sex and P.D.A. Typical Mexican music is sexually charged, filled with hip gyrations. Romance and movement fill every Mexican festival.

Mariachi is a long-standing musical tradition that involves a band of 4-12 eccentrically uniformed men, equipped with trumpets and various string instruments, playing impressively synchronized romantic serenades for diners and party guests. Mariachi bands can be found in public squares offering their services, or for hire at parties and special celebrations. It is typical to see Mariachi bands at weddings, birthday parties, and family reunions in Mexico. Mariachi bands

are essentially seductive serenades for hire. If you have the opportunity to attend a Mariachi party, make sure to accept the invitation!

ECONOMY

Mexico's economy is one of the strongest and fastest growing in Latin America. After suffering a major economy crisis with the devaluation of the national currency, the MXN Pesos in 1994, the economy has bounced back and is performing better than ever. The backbone of the economy is a variety of exports and Free Trade agreements with over 40 different countries.

Unfortunately, economic inequality in Mexico is painfully apparent. The world's richest man, Carlos Slim, who made his fortune in the telecommunications industry, and some of the world's poorest residents live under the same flag. Over 50 percent of Mexico's population lives in poverty.

The division between the rich and the poor is evident everywhere you go in Mexico. The rich dine in international restaurants, have summerhouses in Acapulco and Cuernavaca, vacation to Las Vegas and Miami, and enjoy all the luxurious amenities that life has to offer. The poor in Mexico live in a very different world. Their diet is comprised of plain tortillas, beans, and Coca-Cola. Their children drop out of school to work at painfully young ages. They struggle with malnutrition and treatable health problems that are left untreated.

Most people are not aware of the staggering wealth that exists in Mexico, outside of Slim. There are neighborhoods in Mexico City where I have seen decadence unlike any major city I have visited. Sante Fe, one of the major business districts in the city, is home to the headquarters of major companies like Cisco, Tel Cel, Kraft, Univison, Samsung, ect. Skyscrapers shoot up next to very poor barrios that are built on a garbage dump. Despite all of the recent economic successes, it clearly has only benefited a minority of the population.

The Mexican economy can be difficult to gauge because so much of it is informal. As of 2013, 59 percent of Mexico's laborers comprise the informal economy. Included are people who operate food stands, work as mechanics, street cleaners, artisans, and just about any kind of hustle you can imagine. For this reason, statistics that attempt to gauge unemployment or daily wages are hard to pinpoint.

For information on where you might fit in the Mexican economy, check out the Cost of Living section.

Disparity Unrevealed, the Tale of two Lomases

I had a recent experience that may demonstrate the economic inequality better. I felt as if I had set foot in two entirely different words, ironically both by the same name. In the morning, I went to visit a community center in Lomas de San Isidrio. On the outskirts of the city, many homes in the community have no electricity or running water.   One of the main projects of the non-profit I have worked with is assisting families by building gardens in their backyard, so they can save money on food, eat healthier, and always have access to fresh produce. We happened to arrive on market day, when families lay out their modest produce for sale. I talked to a woman in the community who shared that she tries to buy all that she needs for the week at the market because it is much cheaper than buying produce at smaller stores on a daily basis. *"I try to buy my tomatoes a little inmaduro (unripe) so they will last the whole week. I can get them for 12 pesos a kilo($1) at the market, and if I buy them every day at the store it might cost me 20 - 25 pesos ($1.80 - $2.10). So it's important to take advantage of the prices at the market!"*

Later that night, a friend invited me to go to a wine tasting in a neighborhood called InterLomas de Chapultepec. Her friend was the event coordinator for a boutique that specializes in Mexican wines. The boutique organized a tasting with friends to sell the surplus wine from the previous season. I love wine, so I gladly accepted.

InterLomas is known as one of Mexico City's wealthiest neighborhoods. Sprawling mansions peek out over protective walls. You feel like you're in a wealthy neighborhood of an

LOCAL STORY

In the seat across from me on the metro was a man with a kind, leathery face that looked like it has been rapidly aged by decades of arduous physical labor. His hair said he was 50, but the wrinkles in his face and hands suggested 75. He leaned back in his seat and closed his eyes, moving helplessly with the jerky motions of the train, looking like he just put in a 12-14 hour day of labor.

His hands were caked with car grease and he had cement residue on his tattered jeans. Around his neck was a yellow Spongebob Satchel. He reached into the sachel and pulled out a handful of coins, proceeding to slowly count them and transfer the count from one hand to another, barely opening his eyes as he did so.

On one of the stops, a group of four boarded the train. One of them looked about 7 months pregnant, the other was holding a toddler in her arms and another small child by her side. The toddler had a runny nose and dirt on his brow and cheeks. The pregnant girl made an announcement, she said they were living on the street, trying to scrape together enough to survive. They sang together, poorly, but I had to give them some credit for trying.

As they finished singing, the little girl made her way down the aisle, collecting coins from those willing to part with a peso. She passed the man with the Spongebob satchel and he stopped her, and placed a 5 peso coin in her hand, smiling so wide it looked like the wrinkles in his face would crack.

It was a simple gesture that I'm sure went mostly unnoticed. The smile on his face when he parted with one of his precious pesos was so powerful.

No matter how dire your situation, there's always someone among you with less, who could use your help.

American suburb. At the wine tasting, we tried eight different wines, with price-tags ranging from 170 - 880 pesos a bottle ($14 - $75). We were served fine cheese and Italian meats with fresh baguettes. The person leading the tasting went on in great detail about how remarkably priced the wines were for their quality.

He gave us suggestions of what meats and spices to pair with the respective wines, meticulously analyzing the unique scents, tastes and evoking sensations. To close the tasting, he said, *"Anyone who chooses a bottle of wine based on price, doesn't know anything about wine."* The audience nodded in agreement.

As I left the tasting, I thought to myself, these two Lomas communities, slightly more than an hour apart in this sprawling city, are completely different worlds. No one in InterLomas has ever had to worry about buying their tomatoes all at once to save 12 pesos a kilo. No one in Lomas de San Isidrio has ever had to decide what goes better with their steak, a Shiraz or Cabernet Sauvignon? Most of them only enjoy meat on very special occasions. They certainly wouldn't consider spending 200 pesos on a bottle of wine, probably half their weekly salary, *"a good deal."*

CULTURE

"The greatest reward and luxury of travel is to experience everyday things as if for the first time."

~ Bill Bryson

During my first visit to the city of Oaxaca, about three months after I moved to Mexico, I laid in the bed of my hostel and was soon awakened by sounds of a marching band or something that sounded a great deal like a marching band.

It was like I had stumbled upon a Mardi Gras Parade. It was midnight, mind you, and I saw about 200 people in the streets, a handful of them wearing absurdly enormous costumes. They twirled in the streets to the beat of

Familia O'Grady 2014

drums and trumpets. As I scanned the group, I noticed I wasn't the only one who had been roused out of bed. Neighbors lined the streets, clapping to the music and smiling. Some of them held prepared food and drinks that they passed out to the crowd for free.

An old man approached me with a steaming cup of Champurrado (cinnamon flavored hot chocolate) and insisted I take it. "What is going on?" I asked him. He smiled and said, "We're celebrating Santa Lucia! Every month we celebrate a saint and today is Santa Lucia!" I followed the parade with him, still dressed in my pajamas, without apology, thinking to myself how glad I was that I got out of bed to enjoy the celebration. I told the hot chocolate compadre that this was my first time in Oaxaca. He leaned over and said, *"I have lived all over Mexico, but here in Oaxaca, the culture is the best. Best food, best party, best people, just the best! You've come to the right place!"* In that moment, I couldn't help but agree.

The encounter helped me realize how proud Mexicans are of their culture. Every state has their customs and traditions. There is an air of competitiveness between regions, competing for who has the most to offer. In general, there is no broad brushstroke you can cast over the culture in Mexico. Vibrant and passionate are words that come to mind when describing Mexican culture. Just when you think you've seen it all, Mexico will surprise you. No matter where you are, you are guaranteed to come across something different and unique.

My experiences with Mexicans have been nothing but positive and it's one of the best parts about living in this country without a doubt. Most Mexicans are eager to prove the negative reputation of their country as overrun by violence, drugs, poverty and dilenquency wrong.

There's something about the Latin American spirit that makes me feel I was born in the wrong country and have just arrived home. The warmth and passion makes you feel welcome.From the guy selling tacos on the corner who you quickly befriend, to the people you work with and the friends you meet along the way.

Ahora / Ahorrita (right now, now)

The ambiguous distinction between these two words speaks volumes as to the relaxed nature of Mexican culture. "Ahora" as you might know, means "right now", where as ahorrita, means essentially the same thing but in such a general sense you can never be quite sure what to expect. For example, if the cable guy says he will come install the internet modem "ahora", then presumably, he will be getting to his car within the next hour and it will be done by the end of the day. If he says it will be done "ahorrita", then it could be tomorrow, next week, or sometime before the next presidency. You just never know.

GAY & LESBIAN

Like the United States, laws on same sex marriage in Mexico vary on a state-by-state basis. At the time of writing, same sex marriages are allowed in Mexico City, Oaxaca, Quintana Roo, Cohuilia and Colima. Still, that is only five out of 31 states throughout the country. In general, rural areas are still dominated by a machismo culture that is very resistant to change. Mexico City has a thriving gay & lesbian community concentrated in a great neighborhood called Zona Rosa, near the center of the city. The gay pride parade is the second largest in Latin America.

FOOD

"I've seen zero evidence of any nation on Earth, other than Mexico, even remotely having the slightest clue what Mexican food is about or even come close to reproducing it. It is perhaps the most misunderstood country and cuisine on Earth."

~ Anthony Bourdain

Mexico is famous for its amazingly diverse gastronomy. Anthony Bourdain said it best. You may think you've had Mexican food, but you really haven't until you've set foot in Mexico for the real thing. Food in Mexico is flavorful, heavy, and cheap. You'll be amazed how many specialties are conjured up with the creative variations of tortilla, beans, cheese, and every kind of meat imaginable. In general, Mexican food isn't vegetarian friendly. There certainly aren't mean substitutes. You could, however, enjoy fajitas, rice, and beans with everything except the meat.

The saying "Don't judge a book by its cover," couldn't be more applicable then when describing the food-scene in Mexico. I've eaten at rustic restaurants with plastic furniture and painfully tacky décor that exposed me to incredible food that has kept me coming back. If you live in fear of getting sick and only dine at facilities that mirror the US or Canada, then you'll be missing out on the very best of Mexican food. As a general rule, if a place is crowded, chances are it's worthy of your taste buds.

Street food has its own culture in Mexico. It's like a living, breathing entity that plays a central role in Mexican society. In any sizable town or city in Mexico, streets are lined with food vendors offering cheap and delicious Mexican delicacies. There are so many options and variations, it can be overwhelming. Which is why we have included an overview, Street Food 101.

Street Food 101

♦ **Tacos:**

The Mexican taco is simple, yet refined. It consists of a small, double layered corn tortilla with meat of any variety, topped with onions, cilantro, lime and your choice of sauce, varying in their lethality. When I say Mexicans will put anything in a taco, I mean it. The cow is a sacred beast, and not one part of the animal goes to waste when it comes to tacos. Brain tacos (sesos), eyes (ojos), stomach (tripa), tongue (lengua) are all popular taco fillings at stands across Mexico. Don't worry, they have non-fear factor meat options as well.

For those with sensitive stomachs, you might want to stick with tacos al pastor, the most popular. Tacos al pastor is a huge slab of meat rotating on an open flame, thinly carved off into your taco and topped with a slice of pineapple. You can't go wrong.

♦ Tortas:

This is essentially the Mexican version of a sandwich. Served on a white roll and filled with anything you can imagine. My favorite is the Hawaiian, with ham, cheese, avocado, pineapple and chile.

♦ Quesadillas:

Contrary to popular belief, quesadillas don't necessarily have to include (cheese). Fresh pressed corn tortillas, filled with anything you want. I love them with zucchini flower and cheese.

♦ Huaraches:

Also the word for sandals, Huaraches are large oval-shaped tortillas filled with beans and covered with cheese, lettuce, tomatoes, salsa and your choice of meat or egg.

♦ Pambazos:

Essentially, a cardiac-arrest sandwich. But man, what a way to go! It is comprised of a soft roll dipped in sauce and lightly fried. Then it's filled with potatoes, lettuce, tomatoes, cream and shredded meat or chorizo.

♦ Gorditas:

Aptly titled "the fatty", gorditas are thick, deep-fried tortillas filled with refried beans, then opened up and filled with lettuce, tomatoes, cheese and meat.

♦ Pozole:

A traditional corn soup that dates back to the days of the Aztecs. Large corn kernels, either chicken or pork meat, served with lettuce, onions, oregano, radishes and tostadas.

♦ Tamales:

Aside from tacos and quesadillas, tamales may be the next most recognized representative of Mexican culinary culture. Moist corn cakes, wrapped in either banana leaf (oja de platano), or corn husk (oja de maiz), then garnished with a variety of fillings. The most popular are tamales Oaxaqueños with mole, chicken, cactus (nopal), cheese, and either red or green sauce.

I could write an entire book on street food in Mexico. It's very difficult to provide a general outline of "Mexican Food", because the cuisine varies a lot from region to region. To put it modestly, Mexico is an amazing place to be if you like to eat. In sizable cities and tourist destinations, there is a variety of international food to fill those non-Mexican cravings.

Seafood Sundays

There's something about Sunday's and seafood in Mexico. It's almost like their version of Sunday - Funday! Mexican families across the country venture out to their favorite seafood restaurant and gorge on their favorite delicacies from the sea. Popular seafood joints are simple, no frills establishments that, on Sundays, pack them in serving up fresh and affordable seafood soup, fried fish, and shrimp cocktails.

Day at the Market

A Mexican Market is a beautiful thing. Food vendors from every corner of the region arrive to sell their products. All cities and towns have at least one permanent market where you can find anything you need. The prices are substantially cheaper than supermarkets, and you are directly supporting the farmers, rather than some international conglomerate.

When you take your first steps into an indoor market, be prepared for sensory overload. Navigating your way through the labyrinth of stalls, hallways, and smells can be overwhelming- slabs of raw meat and fish on ice, mounds of whole chickens being plucked and trimmed at a dizzying pace, fumes of sizzling mole, huge vats of carnitas (fried pork chunks), and deep fried tacos dorados being served up to ravenous customers. And the sounds! One vendor trying to drown out another, luring you over to their stall, slicing off samples of avocado, cheese, and meat to prove that their product is indeed superior. "Blondie, try my avocado. It's the best! Take one!" It's almost like a stock trading floor when the bell sounds, minus the assholes in expensive suits.

DRINKING

Mexicans love to drink and have surprisingly high tolerances considering their less-than-imposing stature. I consider myself a capable drinker and I struggle to keep up with my Mexican counterparts. However, public drunkenness is certainly frowned upon in Mexico. It's seen as a lower-class behavior. So make

special occasion, the alcohol flows!

Cantinas

There are bars and pubs in Mexico just like anywhere else in the world, but if you're feeling adventurous, it pays to explore the age old tradition of the Mexican Cantina. Cantinas are old-school

sure and get ahold of yourself! I'm always amazed by the amount of drinking that goes on at family gatherings. When three generations of Mexicans get together to celebrate a

drinking saloons that are open during the day and usually offer free botanas, or snacks, with your drinks! Generally speaking, authentic cantinas are not what you'd call classy establishments, nor are they date destinations. No sir, there are no apple martinis served. If someone offers to buy you a drink at a cantina, before accepting, know that once you commit to joining a drinking circle, you're in it for the long haul. It's considered very disrespectful to leave once the drinking has commenced. You're there until the bottle is empty or the money is gone, whichever happens first.

What to Drink

◆ **Cerveza (Beer)**

Stay thirsty my friends. Beers like Dos XX and Corona and available all over the world. In fact, beer is Mexico's 17th most lucrative export. Victoria, Indio, Tecate, and Sol are some of the most popular and readily available beers in Mexico. My personal favorite is Bohemia, which is available in light, dark, and weizen editions. In the past couple years there has been a respectable artisan beer scene developing across larger cities.

◆ **Mezcal & Tequila**

What's the difference? All tequilas are mescals but not all mescals are tequilas. Tequila is required, by law, to be produced with Blue Agave Mezcal can be produced with over 30 variety of agave, plus they are made differently. Tequila is most commonly mass produced in autoclaves (large pressure cookers). Mezcal is usually handcrafted, with a few exceptions, cooked in an underground pit lined with volcanic rock which then cooks the Agave leaves for days, caramelizing them.

Tequila basks in all the international shine, but it's a clear cut geographic separation in Mexico. Your drink of choice is a matter of where you're from.

◆ **Pulque**

Pulque is a thick, milky, foamy, drink made by fermenting the sap of the Maguey plant. Served in its original form, the taste is a bit sour and the alcohol content is around 6-8 %. Bars that serve pulque are called Pulquerias and are relatively hard to come by. There are only a handful that I know of in Mexico City.

LANGUAGE

I spoke fluent Spanish when I moved to Mexico. It didn't take me long, however, to realize that my Spanish from Spain was not the same as Mexican Spanish. I've been here over a year and I'm still adjusting. Mexican Spanish is peppered with slang that is unique to the region where it is spoken. Just as people from 'the south' in the United States tend to speak with a heavy twang when compared with those from the west, so too do Mexicans.

Since Mexico shares a border with the U.S., many folks have some exposure to English, whether it is through formal schooling or watching American movies. Their ability level is often associated with their socio-economic class. Many Mexicans who were raised in the private school system were taught by talented English teachers, and as a result, speak decent English. Mexicans that went to public schools, and in many cases didn't finish their schooling, usually don't speak much English.

As is the case with any foreign country, you'll have a much easier time assimilating if you know the language. There are expat communities in parts of Mexico where I'm sure you could get by with a very basic level of Spanish. These areas cater year-round to the expat community, and have adapted to a more

American way of life. For me, part of the beauty of living in another country is immersing yourself in new experiences, socializing with new circles, and trying new things. Each person is seeking their own experiences with unique needs and goals, so my preference may not be yours. That being said, no matter what level you are at, making an effort to learn and improve your Spanish will make a world of difference in your everyday Mexican life.

It's important to note here that there are 62 indigenous languages spoken in Mexico. States like Chiapas, Oaxaca, and Guerrero have large indigenous populations and in rural indigenous communities, many people don't speak a lick of Spanish.

Slang

In the Spanish-speaking world, Mexicans are known for their slang. If you speak the Spanish you learned in a different country, it will take you a little while to adjust. Expect a few awkward misunderstandings. For example, when my friend tried to tell her Spanish speaking hosts that her husband likes eggs for breakfast and instead told them that she liked to eat her husband's balls!

RELIGION

A common response to the question, "How are you?" is, "Muy bien, Gracias a Dios," (Very good, thanks be to God). Mexico is a very religious country and they will attribute almost anything good that happens to them to praising God. Religion plays a major role in Mexican culture. That infamous Catholic guilt has its say in all relationships. The table below is as current as the 2000 census.

describe you, Mexican churches are pretty amazing to see. Pop your head in when the church is

Whether you live in a large city or tiny pueblo, life stops on Sundays for church. Hoards of people, dressed to impress, head for mass with their extended families. It's quite the sight. Afterwards, the gathered families often go out to eat or have a celebratory meal/party at one of their homes.

Even if religious is not an adjective used to

empty and take in the gorgeous hand marble, stained glass, and hand painted ceilings. Their sheer aesthetic beauty and historical importance make them worth a few minutes.

In Mexico City, there are a few neighborhoods with sizable Jewish populations, but not enough to make a percentage in the 2000 census.

CLIMATE

Mexico is a huge country with an amazingly diverse environmental landscape, so naturally the climate varies quite a bit depending on your location. No matter where you are, you are almost guaranteed blue skies and sunshine. If you are in the capital of Mexico City, temperatures usually teeter between 55-65 F (13 - 18 C) in the winter months and 65-80 F (18 - 27 C) in the spring and summer. The same is true for cities like Puebla, Queretaro, San Cristobal de las Casas, San Miguel de Allende and Guanajuato, that find themselves at relatively high elevations. For destinations on the Pacific and Caribbean Coasts, as well as the tropical region of Chiapas, temperatures are pretty much sweltering all-year-long.

Throughout the country, there is a rainy season that pummels the land four-five months a year. The good news is it usually is very predictable. In Mexico City, the rain comes every day like clockwork, between 3-5pm in the afternoon. After the rain subsides, the sun comes back out to bless the rest of the day. On the flip side, coastal regions can get hammered by hurricanes during the rainy season. For some, it's a small price to pay to live in a beach paradise. I suppose it comes with the territory.

Coming from the oppressive east coast winters in Massachusetts and New York, the climate in Mexico is absolutely ideal. Sunny and 75 F all year-round! The rainy season can grow tiresome, but just keep in mind that it doesn't last forever.

NATURE

Mexico offers just about every kind of landscape and ecosystem you could want. Tropical jungles, white sand beaches, mountains, volcanoes, deserts, forests, this country really has it all. The most amazing thing about Mexico's landscape is the proximity between one distinct landscape and another. For example, residents of Mexico City enjoy a temperate climate year-round because of the city's elevation, but are a 4-5 hour drive away from tropical beaches in Acapulco and Veracruz. Chiapas, Mexico's second largest state, is home to beaches, jungles, mountains, and volcanoes! You can spend the morning in the chilly mountain town of San Cristobal de las Casas, take a bus to the city of Palenque, and 6 hours later you can hike through tropical jungle surrounded by monkeys, or search for hot springs and waterfalls in a Zapatista village!

For more information about Mexico's natural assets, see the regional sections.

TIP

"Most people assume that Mexico is a dry hot desert from what they have seen in the movies filmed in the North. The rest of the country, including Guadalajara, has a significant rainy season during the US summer. If you expect summer to be hot, you will not find that in Central Mexico."

~ Katherine MacKintosh, expat from Tennessee living in Guadalajara

TRANSPORTATION

Transportation varies between large city and rural area.

◆ **In the city**

Mexico City has one of the best public transportation systems in the world, with the most expansive metro system world-wide. It does it all without breaking the bank, at about 40 cents per ride. There is also a Metrobus system that runs several routes throughout the city, occupying its own lane so it is not at the mercy of traffic.

While it's relatively easy to get anywhere you need to with public transportation, it doesn't mean you'll be comfortable. Imagine the most crowded bus or train you have ever ridden. Ok, now add 3-4 morbidly obese men and a few Chihuahuas and you've got buses in Mexico during rush-hour. It's really unexplainable until you're squished up against the window, suffocating from the stench of way too much cologne and hair gel. Getting on and off the bus during rush hour is an experience akin to the Running of the Bulls in a pin-ball machine. But hey, I'm not complaining. It will get you from A to B. If you're easily claustrophobic, it might be best to grab a taxi.

Smaller cities and towns usually rely on smaller buses, or combis, that circulate various routes with erratic frequency.

◆ **Taxis**

Taxis are readily available across the country, but you need to use caution. There have been cases of groups dedicated to kidnapping using taxis as a way to pick up unsuspecting tourists, locals, or anyone who looks like they have money, then extorting them for their release. I must stress this is not a common occurrence, but it does happen. Most cities have stands called "Radio Taxis," that are more secure and employ drivers that have been vetted and approved. They tend to be more expensive than street taxis but the few extra pesos are worth the peace of mind, especially if you're taking a cab at night.

◆ **Bus**

Prior to moving to Mexico, I'd spent time living in Central America, so I assumed that I would see the same old, dilapidated "Chicken Buses." These would allow me to take a 6 hour trip for $5 and there was a good chance I would have to share a seat with a farm animal. Not the case! Buses in Mexico are very nice and comfortable (think Peter Pan, Greyhound or Megabus), but relatively expensive, even compared to the U.S.!

For example, a 6 hour bus ride from Mexico City to the beach city of Acapulco will cost you about $45 one-way. There are four bus terminals in Mexico City that offer transportation to just about anywhere in the country. The most popular bus companies are ADO, ELN, Omnibus, Primera Plus and Estrella de Oro.

♦ **Airplane**

In the past few years, discount airline carriers <u>Vivaaerobus</u> and <u>Volaris</u> have popped up to offer very affordable airfare to national destinations. If you book at the right time, you can find a steal! I just booked a ticket from Mexico City to Guadalajara (which would be a 9-hour bus ride) on Vivaaerobus for less than $100 round trip.

Depending on where you're headed, it makes sense to compare prices of buses with discount airlines it might be worth spending a couple hundred pesos more to avoid an exceedingly long, but surprisingly comfortable, bus ride.

♦ **Driving in Mexico**

I've heard people say, if you can drive in Mexico, you can drive anywhere in the world. I think it's true. Drivers in Mexico seem to be constantly engaged in a vehicular pissing contest. The classic Mexican machismo definitely comes into play behind the wheel. If you decide to rent or buy a car in Mexico, be aware the driving culture is most likely different from the one

Familia O'Grady 2014

you are accustomed to. Stoplights are liberally interpreted to say the least as are speed limits. I also joke that despite how safe I feel in Mexico, my most exposed moments are when I am crossing the street.

Deciding if owning a vehicle is necessary depends on your personality and where you choose to live. Big cities like Monterrey, Guadalajara, Puebla and Mexico City have ample public transportation options for both internal and long distance travel. Because of traffic, owning a car can sometimes be more of an inconvenience than a necessity. However, if you are looking for the small town experience, a vehicle is a must in order to get the kind of freedom and mobility you want.

Driving your own wheels also provides the added bonus of access to countless little-known destinations, off the beaten road, that are not accessible by public transportation. If you're an avid explorer, renting or purchasing a car might be the best option for you.

♦ Police/Traffic Stops

In the interest of full disclosure, there is undoubtedly profiling by cops against white foreigners who are driving in Mexico. I've heard stories from friends who have gotten pulled over for no particular reason, supposedly because a policeman was looking for a bribe, or *Mordida*. However, to provide some perspective, in the United States, I've heard many stories regarding unnecessary traffic stops of those driving with Colorado plates, outside of Colorado, since they legalized marijuana. The major difference is one is institutionalized and the other is off the books.

«IMMIGRATION»

Mexico is known as an emigrant nation. Because of its close proximity to the "EL Norte," both Canada and the United States receive hundreds of thousands of Mexican immigrants annually. The United States currently estimates there are 12 million Mexican immigrants in the US, accounting for over 30 percent of its entire immigrant population.

The steady rise of the Mexican economy in recent years has opened new doors in Mexico as an emerging land of opportunity. Since the NAFTA trade agreement was signed between Mexico, the U.S., and Canada in 1994, opportunities have emerged for multi-national corporations in Mexico, creating attractive job opportunities for foreigners.

From 2000 to 2010, the foreign-born population living in Mexico nearly doubled. Americans comprise of about 75% of that population. Over one million live and work in Mexico. Whether you are a retiree looking to stretch your dollar, an entrepreneur looking to start a business with less start up capital, or simply an adventurer looking for a change of scenery, Mexico is becoming an increasing attractive place for a number of reasons. This Mexican re-start is not without hoops. Below you will learn what paths exist to a life in Mexico.

Tourist / Business Visa

Immigration rules vary depending on your intentions and needs. You need to ask yourself, "How long do I plan on staying in the country at any one time?" and "What will I be doing?" On a tourist or business visa, you are allowed up to 180 days in the country. No formal application is required for North Americans to obtain these visas. You will simply fill out a form when you arrive in Mexico and declare how long you will be staying. I recommend staying in Mexico for at least 6 months before you decide if you want to make the move permanent.

Why bother with a Visa?

If your goal is to "snow-bird" and escape the brutal winters from the north, living in Mexico a few months out of the year, you will probably be fine living on a tourist visa. However, if you hope to settle down permanently in Mexico, you will need to apply for a temporary resident visa, or FM-3.

The ABC's of Residency

Visitante, the FMM (Tourist Visa)– This is the common card issued to all tourists upon their arrival in Mexico. It allows you up to 180 days in the country.

Make sure not to lose the card, as you will need it to exit the country!

Residente Temporal, the FM-3 (Temporary Resident)- You will need this if you plan to stay in Mexico longer than six months. It is also necessary if you plan on working while in Mexico or opening a Mexican bank account. The FM-3 must be renewed on an annual basis.

Residente Permanente, formerly the FM-2 (Permanent Visa)- The FM-2 is the visa required for permanent residency or Mexican citizenship. There are two types of FM-2 visas: one allows you to work in Mexico, and the other, Rentista Visa, is for retirees living on their own income. This gives you most of the rights of a Mexican citizen, with the exception of voting.

Visitante, formerly the FMM (Forma Migratoria Multiple) for Tourists

When you arrive at a Mexican airport (usually on the plane) they will give you the FMM along with a customs declaration form. It is VERY IMPORTANT that you hold on to the form, called an FMM! They will not allow you to leave Mexico without it. I can't stress this enough. The importance of this form is merely mentioned in passing on the plane and can be easy to miss, especially if you don't speak Spanish. It can turn into a travel nightmare, as it did for me when I first came to Mexico to interview for my current job.

Residente Temporal, formerly the FM-3

If you plan to stay in Mexico f-or more than 6

months continuously, or desire certain rights that are granted to temporary residents, you will want to apply for temporary residency, formerly the FM-3 visa. The visa should cost about $3,200 Pesos ($250 USD) and is good for one year before it has to be renewed.

If you're applying for residente temporal as a retiree, you must prove that you can support yourself financially. The monthly requirement for retirees is $2,000 USD in net income per month. If you own property in Mexico then your income requirements are halved. This can be accomplished through social security benefits, a pension, or a combination of the two. Or, you can provide bank statements or investment receipts that show an average balance of $100,000 for the past 12 months or $200,000 in property.

If you are planning to apply for the FM-3 work visa, you will need a letter from your employer stating your position and salary you will be receiving.

As of November 1st, 2012 you must initiate this process from a Mexican consulate outside of Mexico. The process includes an interview by an immigration agent. If they determine you are not a drug smuggler, fugitive, or hold other malicious intent, and you can prove financial solvency, you'll be granted a temporary 90 day visa on your passport, which you'll use in the interim, then finalize the application process at an Instituto Nacional de Migración in Mexico City, Monterrey, or Guadalajara.

You will need to renew this visa annually. After four years carrying a residente temporal card, you will be eligible for a residente perminente, unless you are married to a citizen, then it only takes two years to become eligible for perminente.

You can apply for the visa in person, or you can hire a legal representative to file for you. If you can afford an attorney, and despise the idea of enduring one exceedingly tedious bureaucratic procedure after another, then I would say pay up. It's like having one of those VIP passes at an amusement park that lets you cut lines on all of the rides. However, immigration lawyers aren't cheap. They can cost between $500-$1,000, and that's on top of the $300 you'll be paying for the visa.

Document Checklist

»   FMM tourist card that you received upon entry to Mexico

»   Your original passport and one copy of the front page of your passport

»   1 passport-sized photo without wearing glasses

»   A Comprobant Domicillio, or p address. This ca receipt for internet, electricity, or other utility bill. Something to prove you have an address in Mexico.

»   If you plan on working, you will need a letter from your employer stating how much you will be paid.

Citizenship

Unless you qualify for one of the exceptions listed below, you must hold a FM-2 Visa for at least four years before you can apply for Mexican citizenship. If you are a U.S. citizen, you can hold dual-citizenship, you aren't required to renounce your U.S. citizenship. Thereby, granting you both passports and the privileges awarded to you as a citizen of both countries.

Alternate Paths to Residency

♦ First Degree Relatives

The quickest way to acquire Mexican citizenship is if you have parents or siblings that were born in Mexico. These blood relatives allow you to circumvent all of the other steps in the process and cut to the front of the line. All you need is a copy of your parent's original birth certificate.

♦ Marriage

Aside from Mexican parents or siblings, the express ticket to Mexican citizenship is to fall in love and find yourself a Mexican spouse. If you have lived in Mexico with an FM-2 Visa for two years and are married to a Mexican citizen, you can apply for Mexican citizenship. The process usually takes about three months.

Where to Start?

Reading, researching, and preparing documents for the immigration process will undoubtedly leave you cursing bureaucracy. Every consulate varies a bit on their interpretation of the current requirements and procedures. On the bright side, you'll have plenty of time to make new friends while waiting in line at the Immigration Office. Start by calling your nearest consulate and get their list of requirements, required documents, and procedure. Try to get the name of the agent you speak with and make every effort to continue the process with the same agent. I emailed the consulate in Houston and simply wrote, "I want to retire in Mexico. What forms do I need to fill out?" Within an hour I was given the following response:

Requirements for temporary residence

1. Passport (original and copy of the page with your personal details and photograph

2. 1 Picture (Passport size, front and no glasses)

3. If the visitor is not an American citizen, then he must provide proof of legal stay/residence in the US

4. Financial solvency

a) Letter from your bank or financial institution stating that you have had investment funds or savings of at least $100,621 USD and provide the related bank statements for the last 12 months in which that amount is reflected. The bank letter (original) must include the applicant's complete name, bank account number and balance for the last 12 months and it has to be signed by the branch manager.

Or,

b) Prove that you have a monthly income of at least $2,012 USD.

In order to prove income, you can provide your pay-stubs for the last 6 months or the letter from Social Security stating the monthly amount that you will be receiving and the related bank statements in which reflected at least $2,012 USD.

Requirements for permanent residence

1. Passport (original and copy of the page with your personal details and photograph

2. 1 Picture (Passport size, front and no glasses)

3. If the visitor is not an American citizen, then he must provide proof of legal stay/residence in the US.

4. Financial solvency

a) Letter from your bank or financial institution stating that you have had investment funds or savings of at least $125,776 USD and provide the related bank statements for the last 12 months in which that amount is reflected. The bank letter (original) must include the applicant's complete name, bank account number and balance for the last 12 months and it has to be signed by the branch manager.

Or,

b) Prove that you have a monthly income of at least $2,515 USD.

In order to prove income, you can provide your pay-stubs for the last 6 months or the letter from Social Security stating the monthly amount that you will be receiving and the related bank statements in which reflected at least $2,515 USD.

Once you have your complete documents, you can send another email to book an appointment. (atencionpublicohou@sre.gob.mx)

While there are many hoops to jump through, the good news is once you're past the paperwork, it's relatively easy to obtain residency in Mexico. Especially when compared to what Mexicans have to go through to gain residency in the U.S. or Canada.

«WHERE TO SETTLE?»

Find out where in Mexico will satisfy your needs and provide the lifestyle you seek

Finding your slice of heaven is all about prioritizing. This section will guide you to the region that will satisfy your needs and provide you with the lifestyle you are looking for.

In the **Basics** section, you learned about the drastic natural, environmental, and social diversity that makes choosing where to settle a daunting decision. Not to worry! I will do my best to enlighten you with the pros and cons of the best expat destinations in Mexico. The information is based on my own experiences in addition to numerous expat interviews with those who have found happiness and a sense of community in their regions of choice.

The first step is to ask yourself a few simple questions, "What am I looking for? What is most important to me? What can't I live without? What are deal breakers?" Nailing down answers to these questions will help narrow the search for your Mexican paradise.

A great way to organize and prioritize your thoughts is by using the C.A.S.S. system: Climate, Activities/Amenities, Setting, and Social Requirements.

CLIMATE

Contrary to popular belief, there are regions in Mexico that aren't jalapeño hot and sunny 365 days a year. That being said, if hot and sunny is what you're looking for, there are countless beach havens that span across the 9,330 kilometers (5,797 miles) of Mexican coastline. The weather along the Pacific,

Caribbean, and Gulf coasts are generally very hot. The same is true for Palenque in Chiapas. If your skin is pasty white like mine, you'll probably want to stock up on premium sun tan lotion, the sun here doesn't joke around! I found that out the hard way.

If you prefer spring weather, with temperatures ranging between 60 and 80 degrees F (15 - 27 C), then Cuernavaca, known as the city of eternal spring, could be your sweet spot. If you prefer something a bit cooler, than perhaps the colonial town San Cristobal de las Casas or San Miguel de Allende would be a better fit. Put a great deal of thought into what your ideal climate is before making a commitment to one region.

The good news is, no matter where you are in Mexico, you're usually only a few hours drive to the coast or the mountains. A short drive or bus ride, and you can escape to a refreshing change of scenery.

ACTIVITIES

What do you enjoy doing to pass the time, or perhaps more importantly, how would you like to pass your time in Mexico? Are you a party animal who wants to master their salsa skills? Maybe all you need is your own sliver of a white sand beach to find your little slice of nirvana.

Is it important for you to be close to a gym to stay active or are you content running on your own through the forest? Are you an avid kayaker, birder, surfer, fisherman(woman)? Whether you're a city slicker or a small town guy/gal, Mexico has a wide range of options to fulfill your needs. I'll give you the run down of activities in each region so you can make the best decision for you.

If you're moving to Mexico as a young adult, you'll probably need to be connected to work and entrepreneurial opportunities. If you're a retiree looking for some peace and serenity, I doubt you'll be comfortable with the Jerry Springer-like spring break crowd in Cancun or Playa del Carmen.

AMENITIES

We're creatures of comfort. What are the comforts you don't want to live without? In larger cities, you won't have trouble finding internet access, reliable electricity, or hot water. However, if you're looking for that small town getaway, or your own off-the-grid finca, your connection to the rest of the world might be spotty at best. But after all, that would be exactly what you're looking for.

Don't forget about food supply. Small towns rely heavily on local markets and corner stores. They have fresh produce and handmade tortillas. However, if you're accustomed to buying fancier, international food products, you might be at a loss in a rural village where hummus, granola, and kale chips are not readily available. Make a list of what is important to have available.

When in doubt you can learn how to make hummus, granola, and other healthy snacks from what you do have handy.

SETTING

Are you coming to Mexico in search of a quaint, beach paradise where you can lie in your hammock all day listening to the sound of the waves? Are you a city slicker who thrives on the chaotic pulse that only a major metropolis can provide? Even within Mexico's biggest cities, you can find relatively peaceful enclaves of tranquility, tucked away from the hustle and bustle of the city. The regional sections will help explain what the setting is like in the various states throughout the country in order to assist you in the daunting task of narrowing down your potential landing zones.

SOCIAL REQUIREMENTS

Whether arriving on your own, with a partner, or with a family, you need to put serious thought into what kind of social life you want to build for yourself. Do you want to be part of a vibrant expat community or are you hoping to dive into the local culture and Mexican-ize yourself? Are you a loner or an extrovert? In Mexico, you'll have the option to build the kind of life you want by surrounding yourself with like-minded people. Over isolation isn't really a problem, since it's relatively easy to position yourself close to a large town or city, even if what you're after is a little separation.

I've really enjoyed making friends with the

locals. It's been an extraordinary way to experience the culture. Within minutes of meeting someone, I've been invited to weddings, dinner parties, and quincineras. Of course, language skills are required.

Another aspect to consider that goes hand in hand with social requirements is living expenses. We will discuss this more in depth in the regional section, but you should have a monthly budget in mind when contemplating which region is right for you since the cost of living can vary quite a bit.

TO SUM UP

Now that you've got an idea of WHAT you want, it's time to zero in on WHERE you'll find it. In the following regional sections, I will shine a spot-light on what life is like across the most popular expat destinations, and in some of the up-and-coming expat destination throughout Mexico.

Before diving into this section, it's important to mention that in order to give you a thorough rundown of the best places to live for expats, I had to be selective. Mexico is enormous and remarkably diverse! The goal of this book is to help you know what to expect when living in Mexico. You'll get an idea of where in this incredible country you'll find your slice of paradise and ultimate happiness, based on the priorities that we mentioned in the previous section.

There are some parts of Mexico that I have elected not to include because they aren't viable places to live as an expat, or maybe they simply aren't on the radar.

There is no shortage of diverse options and environments for any expat in Mexico. Finding the best location for you is all about choices and priorities. You can live in a community full of expats with whom you can speak English, play tennis and golf, join book clubs and artisan groups, and create a life for yourself that will be a more relaxing, stress-free version of the life you are accustomed to at home. The other option is choosing to live amongst the local community, which could entail you making a bit of a sacrifice in terms of services and amenities.

Needless to say, you will have to make a greater effort in terms of speaking Spanish and learning the local culture and traditions in order to integrate into the local community.

It's a personal choice and there is no right answer, just recommendations so you'll know what to expect and be able to make the most out of the experience.

I had the opportunity to connect with Constance Balawender, who has been living in Mexico for over 45 years now. She eloquently articulated the complex, challenging and transformative experience of moving abroad.

"We all enter into any moment in our development based on our own cultural and individual identity. This obviously supports or inhibits our disposition toward thinking and learning in our own culture and society, but highly affects our concepts of truth, beauty, and goodness in other cultures and societies. We must also not disavow economic overlays, that each of us has experienced and which

limit or extend our understanding of different social strata to which we come in contact. Most important are our values, that result from this complexity of identities, toward the meaning of life, and how other individuals live their lives, whether similar or different to our own.

Watching a movie, or reading a novel about any incident or change in the history of any culture, will never replace the actual experience, taken with an open mind, and researching with the intention, to understand what has come before, what are the consequences, what is here and now, and what are those consequences...and not making a judgment which most of us are so eager to put on everything we come into contact with.

Life lived is the total picture, and after living in Mexico for 45 years, I cannot say that my perception of this culture has not changed much, as it has been expanded by the connections and extensions that I have lived, and continue to live every day. I have worked with, and become friends with Mayan women weavers, political movers and shakers, hard-working professionals as myself, multi-millionaires...a broad spectrum of what represents the Mexican culture. It is definitely a mosaic of A to Z, but will always depend upon the disposition of the person who walks into this new and, has-to-be different culture, to understand how the pieces fit."

~ Constance Balawender, expat

«MEXICO CITY»

- *Mexico, Distrito Federal*
- *Population: 21.2 million*
- *Benito Juarez International Airport*
- *More than 150 museums*
- *Largest Public Transport Hub*
- *Largest University in the Americas(UNAM)*

Mexico City is so often overlooked as a travel destination and that really is a crying shame. The city has so much to offer! As someone who has lived in New York, Madrid, and Washington D.C., I can honestly say Mexico City is the best city I have been to thus far.

So many people come to Mexico for the beaches, but if you're a city lover, Mexico City has tons to offer. This city is authentic, beautifully chaotic, and there's never a dull moment. Here are the top seven reasons to consider Mexico City:

1. Museos Galore

Mexico City has more museums per capita than any city in the world. When you consider there are 25 million people in this city, that's a ton of museums!

Every Sunday, all

The last Wednesday of every month is *"Noche de Museos,"* where a handful of museums offer free events and keep their doors upon until midnight.

2. Public Transportation

If I were to make a list of the worst things about living in Mexico City, traffic would be at the top. Fortunately, there's a

museums are free and any other day of the week they're very affordable, averaging $4.

fabulous public transportation system that can bypass this and take you anywhere in the city you desire. I've lived in Washington D.C., New York City and Madrid, and the Mexico City Metro is cleaner than all of them. It's also the cheapest, at about 40 cents per ride. Plus, in public transit you have the chance to be entertained by stand up comedy routines, singing, and blaring music out of giant speakers in backpacks. Or you could purchase anything from candied apples to gum, hammers and razors. Never a dull moment!

3. Parks, *Parques*

This city can feel a little, hmmm, chaotic at times. Fortunately, almost every neighborhood has a park that you can go to escape, play ball, take your dog for a walk, or meet up with a love interest.   There are more than 70 parks in the city, the biggest of which is Parque de Chapultepex. It is made up of over 2,000 hectares and is home to 2 museums, a zoo and a huge castle that overlooks the city. I frequent Parque Viveros and Parque Delta to play basketball and workout on weekends.

4. Market on a Sunday

There's nothing like a Sunday morning in Mexico. A walk to the local market will provide great people watching. You can watch families who visit the market each week for a meal. You can purchase any kind of food you can imagine. Fresh fruit of all kinds, and the vendors will proudly slice off a piece for you to sample in an effort to prove the superior quality of their product. You won't see that at Wholefoods!

The whole ordeal is super entertaining. Vendors shout out to you like auctioneers as you pass by, "Joven, que le damos!!!!!"(Youngin', what can we get you!). They shout out prices and products from all directions. They affectionately call me guero (literally, whitey), everywhere I go. I've gotten used to it. It's endearing.

At the Sunday market, the food selection is remarkable. There's the seafood stand with hot and crispy shrimp empanadas served with avocado and mayo, fried fish fillets, fish tostadas, and shrimp soup. You've got the quesadillas(a personal favorite of mine) deep fried with chicken, cheese, and zucchini flower.

Barbacoa is a breakfast favorite, specifically as a hangover cure. Contrary to popular gringo belief, it does not translate to Barbaque. Barbacoa is slow cooked beef, kinda like brisket but more tender and served in fresh corn tortillas.

5. The Main Plaza, *El Zocolo*

The *Zocolo* refers to the main plaza in any town or city. There's one in every notable town in Mexico.

The Zocolo in Mexico City is the largest one in Latin America and widely considered the most beautiful. The plaza is home to the Santo Domingo Catheral and the Palacio Nacional.

The Cathedral is incredibly beautiful and a common tourist destination. Next to the Cathedral is the Palacio Mayor where the President supposedly works. There are amazing Diego Rivera murals that are open to the public during the week.

Just last week I went to a free concert in the Zocolo. There are always cultural events and expositions in the main plaza that are open to the public.

Surrounding the Zocolo are a number of restaurants and bars where you can enjoy a meal or a cold beer with an incredible view of the entire plaza. If you go, check out the terrace of Puro Corazon. They have killer waffles!

6. Cantinas

Cantinas offer the ultimate drinking experience in Mexico. Boy, do Mexicans know how to drink, they don't mess around. It's the stamina that's impressive.

Go to a cantina in Mexico and you'll see mostly men, depending on what neighborhood you're in, in their suits and ties, socializing over a bottle of tequila. Naturally, the owners of the bar want them to stay and order another bottle of tequila so they bring out plates of delicious food on the house if you order more than 2 drinks. Oftentimes there's a mariachi or some form of musical entertainment. It's so much more fun than any bar I've ever frequented in the US.

There are many classes of cantinas. Some are posh and pricey while others are cesspools of sex and cigarette smoke. Make sure and do your research before venturing in.

7. The Food

Hands down, the most amazing thing about Mexico City and possibly Mexico as a country is the wide array of cheap, delicious, and readily available food. No matter where you are, its hard to walk a block without running into a street vendor. Forty percent of Mexico's entire economy is informal, meaning people run their own businesses from the street. Much of that 40% revolves around food.

You will be blown away by the amount of creative combinations of meat, tortillas and cheese. Food is cheap and bursting with flavor. It's simple, but always delicious. Vegetarians, here is a word of warning. Vegetarianism is not a well understood concept in Mexico, so you will run into challenges if you don't cook for yourself.

This country is much more carnivore friendly.

Breakdown

Mexico City is broken down into delegations and colonias, which are comparable to boroughs and neighborhoods. The city boasts a diversity that allows you to discover something new on a daily basis. In the past few decades, it has emerged as the economic nucleus for Latin America, and that wealth is on display in the business districts like Santa Fe and Polanco, where sleek modern architecture for corporate headquarters and luxurious residences can be found.

I love the international vibe the city exudes, drawing in travelers and expats from around the world. A stroll down the streets in neighborhoods such as Coyocan, La Roma or Condesa will lend you to feel as if you've been transported to a street corner in Barcelona, Paris or Berlin (albeit with a distinct Mexican charm). Foreign languages and cuisines are also easy to come by.

Museum Capital

Mexico City is home to over 170 museums. I've heard it has more museums than any city in the world, but I'm not exactly sure how that can be quantified. Not only are Mexico's museums numerous, but they're the driving force behind the city's thriving cultural and intellectual atmosphere.

The majority of museums charge 60 pesos($4) for entrance during the week and are free on Sundays.

Expat Central

In recent years, Mexico's economic boom and the economic crises in Western

Europe, the United States, Argentina and Venezuela, have resulted in a wave of immigrants arriving in Mexico City. Walking down the street in international neighborhoods such as La Condesa, you're likely to hear a half dozen languages being spoken. It's an amazing place to connect with people from all over the world.

If you're coming to Mexico to work or start a business, Mexico City is the place to be. There are countless opportunities for work that will allow for a comfortable lifestyle. Salaries in Mexico City tend to be much higher than elsewhere in the country, but so is the cost of living, so it all washes out in the end.

Big, Big, Big!

Everything in Mexico City is expansive, numerous, and BIG! Starting with the Zocolo, or main plaza, which is one of the largest public squares in the world. Bordering the Zocolo is the Cathedral Metropolitana, which is the largest church in Latin America. The grandiose records don't stop there. The National Autonomous University of Mexico (UNAM) is the largest University in the Americas with over 250,000 students. The magnificent Bosque de Chapultepec Park is one of the biggest city parks in the world.

Mexico City by the numbers:

» Largest metropolitan area in western hemisphere

» Home to 20 percent of Mexico's entire population

» Home to 700,000 Americans

» National Autonomous University of Mexico (UNAM), is the largest university in the

Americas with over 250,000 students

» Estadio Azteca, the soccer stadium for the Mexican National Team, is the second largest soccer stadium in the world with a seating capacity of 110,000 people

Mexico City is an amazing place. You'll never run out of things to do and you don't have to make the same lifestyle adjustments that you would to move to a smaller, more isolated pueblo. The dining scene is one of the best in the world and museums, concerts, festivals and art exhibitions offer opportunities for you to constantly soak up new knowledge and culture.

However, if you're not accustomed to the megacity lifestyle, it could be a shock. Lucky for you, there are a few destinations just a short bus ride away from the city that offer a more relaxed day-to-day lifestyle, but are

close enough to all the amenities you cherish.

MORELOS

♦ **Cuernavaca, Morelos**

Population: 350,000

Cuernavaca is the capital of the state of Morelos, located about 1 hour outside of Mexico City. It's often referred to as the city of eternal spring for its pleasant temperature year round (60 - 80 F). Many up-class Mexico City residents have second homes in Cuernavaca where they escape on weekends during the rainy season. I certainly wouldn't mind living here year round. They don't call it the city of eternal spring for nothing. The weather here is phenomenal.

Just half an hour away is Jardines de Mexico, the largest flower garden in the world. A great place to stop and smell the roses.

♦ **Tepotzlan, Morelos**

If the thought of a city the size of Cuernavaca is still a bit overwhelming and you're looking for a small town vibe, you might want to check out the magical pueblo, Tepotzlan. Only about a half an hour further from Mexico City than Cuernavaca, Tepotzlan is a picturesque quaint town nestled in a valley with the

Tepotzteco Mountain as a backdrop.

EXPAT EXPERIENCE

"The north of Mexico is too cold for me. San Miguel de Allende is at least 10 to 15 degrees F colder in the winter. Merida is too hot, with high heat and humidity for all but a few months in the winter. Other places are also farther from a direct flight to the US and most of them don't have as good a health system as Cuernavaca. There is a post on our medical care on my blog. Petty crime is high and one needs to be careful but the murder rate consists mostly of drug lords killing other drug lords. Tourists and expats are not the targets nor the victims. There are also over a dozen outstanding schools specializing in teaching Spanish to foreigners. There are more excursion sites and day trips than in many parts of Mexico and buses into Mexico City every ten minutes. Direct buses to the airport every 40 minutes. And we are now just a half hour from Jardines de Mexico, the largest flower garden in the world."

~ James Horn, expat from New York for almost 20 years

Most of the town is lined with character-filled narrow cobblestone streets. On weekends, the town's modest population of 15,000 swells as people escape the chaos of the city and enjoy the town's sprawling market on Sundays.

Tepotzlan is a town that has been dubbed by Mexico's Secretary of Tourism as a *Pueblo Magico*. This is a comprehensive program that has been promoted by federal and state tourism departments to bring attention to the hundreds of beautiful and quaint towns with distinct historical or cultural significance. To qualify for the program, a town must commit to the conservation of cultural symbols, traditions, and architecture.

As far as social requirements go, Tepotzlan has a handful of bars and restaurants and a noticeable number of expats that have integrated into the local community. However, it's close enough to Mexico City (1.5 hours by bus) that you can enjoy the best of both words: a quaint little town where everyone knows each other and access to the bustling Mexico City with all of its entertainment and amenities.

♦ Puebla, Puebla

With a population of 2.9 million, Puebla is the fourth most populous city in Mexico. Despite Puebla's size, its historic district doesn't have the overwhelming chaotic feel of a big city. It's pedestrian friendly and lined with attractive restaurants, bars, and cafes.   What stands out about downtown Puebla is its colorful architecture. There seems to be a church on every corner. They range from relatively unspectacular stone edifices, to audaciously colored Dr. Seuss like sand-drip castles. Not to mention the interiors, which are a spectacle on their own. Adorned with gold leaf, terrifyingly pale Jesus manikins, and biblical paintings on the walls. Each one I saw during my visit was amazingly unique.

The University of the Americas is a bi-lingual University that attracts thousands of international students to Puebla. It also employs hundreds of expat educators.

If you're looking to live in Puebla, you'll want to be as close to the downtown area as possible, so you can be in the heart of the colonial charm.

because it has all the amenities an expat could desire in a nice temperate region. There are *Americanized* and local schools to choose from for those moving with kids and enough museums that an app[1] was created to help guide people to the various attractions. To hear about one family's journey through the local school system in Puebla go to:

http://bit.ly/1HWjtaO

♦ San Pedro Cholula, Puebla

A 15-minute bus ride from Puebla will take you to the expat haven of Cholula. A small town with a sizeable expat population. Cholula has the ominous claim to fame of being home to the largest active volcano in the world, Popcatépetl.

San Pedro Cholula is popular with expats

♦ Queretaro

Queretaro is known throughout the country as the safest state in all of Mexico. This sense of security, as well as a booming industrial economy has made it an attractive destination for expats. It has the advantage of being located smack-dab in the middle of Mexico. I've had the opportunity to spend some time in

---

[1] http://bit.ly/12IarDj

Santiago de Queretaro and the town of Tequisquiapan.

For me, Queretaro is an ideal Mexican City, that's got a lot going for it. Lets start with the location. It's 3 hours by bus to Mexico City, 45 minutes to San Miguel de Allende and 6 hours to either the Pacific or Caribbean coasts.

Then, of course, there's the beautifully moderate year-round climate. Queretaro is without a doubt one of the cleanest and most immaculately designed cities I've ever had the pleasure of visiting.

EXPAT EXPERIENCE

"The most unique thing about Queretaro is the security, beautiful architecture and calmness. Plus Queteraro is located right in the middle of the country, 3 hours to Mexico City, 45 min to San Miguel de Allende, and 90 min to Guanajuato. On the downside, it's the third most expensive city in all of Mexico."

~ Victoria, expat from Spain

Surprisingly, it still flies under the radar, both for Mexicans and expats. Most expats head for the nearby San Miguel because of its notoriety. In recent years, Queretaro has seen an economic boom with regional headquarters being built in the city for companies such as Siemens, Kelloggs, Boeing, and Samsung. This heavy foreign investment has lured Korean, Japanese, American, and German expats to the region.

◆ **Tequisquiapan**

Tequisquiapan is a small, picturesque town about a 40 minute drive from Queretaro. It's similar in size to Tepotzlan, in Morelos. If you're looking for calm, small-town lifestyle, this spot has potential. Tequisquiapan has a beautiful central plaza surrounded by numerous hotels and spas that serve the people of Queretaro and the Mexico City folks who come to this peaceful town on weekends and holidays to escape the rat-race.

EXPAT EXPERIENCE

"I was planning on retirement and I wanted to retire in a place where I could be challenged. I spoke a little Spanish and I knew it was much less to live here. My expenses are probably 25% of what they were in the States (I rent a 3 bedroom house for about $500 a month and pay another $60 a month in utilities).

I did some traveling in Mexico searching for a place to settle. I visted Lake Chapala and found lots of retired military people and kind of a closed minded, conservative ideology. They don't mix with the locals. I wanted to blend in more with the Mexican people.

I love living in Veracruz. People say it is the greenest state in all of Mexico. There is an organic market every Saturday. People are incredibly welcoming, and there are a good amount of expats but not enough that they've taken over the city. It has a very unique and authentic feel. If you keep your eyes and your mind open, there is always something to do."

~ Susan Mills, expat from Dayton Ohio

♦ Veracruz

The history of the state of Veracruz is at the very root of the inception of Mexico as we know it today. It's where Cortez first arrived from Spain. His ship docked in what is now the port of Veracruz and he declared Mexico for the Spanish crown, proceeding to enslave the native people and strip them of their most precious resources. It's always been a strategic import state, acting as the center of Mexico's oil industry and a vital international port which imports and exports goods from around the world.

The state has loads to offer expats. From white sand beaches, jungles, to beautiful cities, ice-capped mountains, and quaint, sleepy little pueblos, Veracruz deserves recognition for its culture and biodiversity. It also offers a very affordable alternative compared to more popular expat destinations.

◆ Xalapa

Walking the street of Xalapa's centro historico, you get the feeling that you've found the perfect medium. A city that has everything you could want in terms of amenities and social offerings; beautiful museums, parks with panoramic views of the colorful city layout, a mountain backdrop, and a world-class music scene. In Xalapa, you're about 3,000 feet above sea level but only a 45 minute drive from the beach. In the downtown area, you'll find a labyrinth of eccentric inclined streets lined with restaurants, cafés, and art galleries.

The University of Veracruz is one of the biggest and most prestigious Universities in Mexico. It has an incredible music program that attracts world-class musicians and

EXPAT EXPERIENCE

" I first came down to Mexico to interview for a job in the Lake Chapala region. I had mixed feelings about the area because it seemed to me like the expats had a closed community and were only interacting with themselves. Everyone spoke English, they have their English-speaking clubs and events, and it just felt too much like America for me. So I kept looking for places to settle and a friend told me I should check out Veracruz. When I discovered the music scene in Xalapa, I knew I would love it here, but I wanted something a bit more quiet and tight knit. I visited Coatepec and it was just a perfect fit. I go to the Symphony in Xalapa every Friday. There is an organic market here on Saturdays. I love the accessibility, the community and of coarse the lower costs of living is a major perk. I pay about $500 a month to rent a two story, three-bedroom house. Can't beat that!"

~ Susan, Coatepec, moved from Dayton, Ohio

has performances 7 days a week. Many of the expats I spoke with said this was one of the major attractions that convinced them to settle in the area. In the course of my interviews with dozens of expats, I've found that being in a place where one can be intellectually stimulated with cultural festivals, music events and museums, is a major priority for people when considering a new place to settle. By those standards, Xalapa is ideal.

◆ Coatepec

Located just 15 kilometers from Xalapa, Coatepec is not quite a suburb, but more like a sister city to Xalapa with a population of around 75,000. The air in Coatepec is crisp and is flavored by the wafting smell of roasting coffee. Many expats are lured to Coatpec by the cultural offerings, tranquil and remarkably affordable living, and the coffee. Veracruz is one of the top coffee producing states in Mexico, and Coatepec is in the heart of it all.

◆ Xico

If the feel of Coatepec is too overwhelming for you and you're more of a small-town guy/gal, you might want to take a look at neighboring Xico. Also donned with the honor *pueblo magico*, Xico is certainly a unique variety. The population is about

EXPAT EXPERIENCE

" We were living and working in Denver and just became bored with the same thing over and over again in small American cities. We had traveled throughout Mexico on a number of occasions, and we decided it would be a great place to settle and stretch our retirement savings. Xalapa looked like a manageable size and we were really struck by its remarkable cultural diversity, with all of the film festivals, dance and musical performances and art galleries. Our living expenses here are about half of what they were in the States. The people are incredibly friendly and welcoming and there is a great expat community that we have connected with."

~ John and Jane, originally from Denver, Colorado.

25,000 and it has a quaint city center, much smaller than Coatepec's but enough amenities to keep you busy.

The jewel of Xico is the breathtaking natural beauty. On the edge of the city, there's a path that will lead you to a jungle hike and an incredible view of mystical waterfalls. It's one of the most incredible natural wonders I've seen in Mexico. To get there from Coatepec, take the bus that says Xico and ask the driver to drop you off at the path to the cascadas.

♦ **Jalisco**

The promotional slogan from Jalisco's State Tourism Secretary says JALISCO

Jalisco

IS MEXICO. Although I think every state will probably try to make the argument that they bleed red, white, and green, there's definitely something iconic about the state of Jalisco.   If you have an image in your mind of what Mexico is like, and what it's known for, you may very well be close to imagining this picturesque town. For starters, two of Mexico's most recognizable cultural icons, tequila and mariachi, come from the state of Jalisco. Just a few decades ago, tequila was a relatively unknown niche drink, and now it's one of the most consumed liquors in the world. The majority of it is produced in the state of Jalisco.

♦ **Guadalajara**

Mexico's second biggest city with a population of about 6 million, Guadalajara offers all of the upsides & amenities for someone looking for an exhilarating urban lifestyle, but at better prices and certainly less chaos than Mexico City.

In Guadalajara, you'll find a beautiful city with a modern infrastructure that blends harmoniously with an ancient architectural layout. It's often called the "Cuidad de Fuentes" because of the prevalence of elaborate fountains and sculptures that grace parks

and public areas throughout the city.   At an altitude of 5,200 feet, the climate in Guadalajara is ideal with temperatures lingering in the 70s and 80s, occasionally peeking in the low 90s in the summer months. The rainy season, between June and September, offers light showers daily in the afternoon and early evenings.

Founded 50 years after Colombus' discovery of the new World, Guadalajara is one of the oldest cities in Mexico. Its rich history is on display in the city's sprawling plazas.

Artisan Capital of Mexico

Like most big cities in Mexico, Guadalajara is divided into six municipalities that make up the city- Tonola, Tlaquepaque, Tlajomulco de Zuniga, El Salto, Zapopan and Guadalajara (yes that would make it Guadalajara, Guadalajara). Tlaquepaque is a happening neighborhood about 30 minutes by bus from downtown. It is famous throughout Mexico as the center for handmade artisan crafts, where you can find anything from the most cliché to the most intricate, unique handicrafts that Mexico has to offer.

"Guadalajara is a beautiful place to live if you like sunshine, a thriving arts and music scene, as well as the traditional Mexican fare of mariachi music and a slower pace of life all within the context of a big city. This lifestyle can be very attractive to expats, and those that stay for the long run, usually do so for the strong friendships that they make here. I recommend Guadalajara to students, recent graduates and retirees. However, it has been my experience that mid-career professionals would be better off in Mexico City for better career opportunities. When looking to make a major move anywhere, I recommend visiting first since everyone has different tastes, but I can assure you that Guadalajara is the most traditional

Mexican city. If th
you're looking for
be disappointed w
Guadalajara."

~ Katherine, originally from Tennessee, lived in Guadalajara for the last five years

Lake Chapala

Expats have been flocking to the shores of Mexico's biggest lake since the early 1900s. Located just an hour outside Guadalajara, it's home to the biggest expat population in Mexico. The main towns along the lake are Ajicic, San Juan de Cosel, Chapala, and Jocotepec. In Ajicic alone, expats comprise about half of the town's population of 16,000. The "Lakeside community" as it is called by locals is a tranquil onclave of Americans, Canadians, and Brits who have carved out their piece the Mexican Dream: cheap property, dirt-cheap quality healthcare, and sunshine.

Today, the shores of Lake Chapala are home to about 40,000 expats, making it the largest expat community in Mexico. While the majority of expats are Americans and Canadians, there are also sizeable amounts of Brits, French, German and Spanish residents who have found refuge on the shores of the Lake. There are a number of different towns in the lakeside area and all of them offer a very different sense of community and lifestyle. I'll break it down for you.

Chapala

Chapala is the largest town on the lake by a long shot, with over 50,000 inhabitants according to the most recent census. The shining jewel of the town is its malecon, or boardwalk,

lining the lake. Accompanied by a park, a market with local handcrafts, street food, and cold beer, it's a blissful place for a romantic stroll or a pensive, solitary walk as the sun goes down. On

EXPAT EXPERIENCE

"A few years ago I said to myself, I can either work until I die or find somewhere where I can afford to live on a fixed budget, so we started to consider the prospects of retiring abroad. Neither of us had been to Mexico before and lets just say we had our doubts. We came down here for an immigration seminar and we bought a house the very same week. It just felt right. The sense of community here is incredible and as far as the setting, it doesn't get much better than this. Sometimes it dawns on us that other people come here for vacation, and we live here! It's hard for me say what my favorite thing is about living on Lake Chapala. All I know is that every morning when we wake up, we're incredibly happy with the decision we made."

~ Kitt and Bill Vincent

either side of the malecon are docks that shoot out into the lake, with boats whose captains are eager to offer you an excursion on their vessel.

The year round expat population in Chapala is between 5,000-7,000 depending on who you ask. Being the oldest expat community in Mexico, it has established support structures to help retirees ease into their new lifestyle.

There's a Red Cross clinic that offers free healthcare for everyone in town. The clinic takes care of most medical needs outside of surgeries, for

TIP

If you're looking to buy property in Ajicic or anywhere on Lake Chapala for that matter, you'll get a much better price if you find a Mexican real estate agent rather than go through an expat office. This can be difficult in Ajicic, as much of the real estate business is currently operated by expats and for expats.

which you'll have to go to the nearest hospital. Medicine and checkups are all free!

An American Legion office is a great resource for the hundreds of veterans that have taken their pensions to Chapala. They provide all kinds of support services.

Ajicic

In Ajicic, you'll find the most concentrated gathering of American and Canadian retirees in Mexico. It's home to over 8,000 expats year-round and as many as 12,000 snow-birders. Driving through the residential streets, you could convince yourself that you've been transported to a suburb in Southern California. The streets are smoothly paved and the lawns perfectly manicured. The Lake Chapala Society is located in Ajijic and provides many expats with assistance. Rents and purchase prices are higher in this village although you can always find a good deal.

I mentioned earlier that some people might be more comfortable in a community where they don't have many adjustments to make in terms of culture, surroundings, and the new language, while others are driven by the challenge of learning Spanish and embracing the culture shock they expect to encounter head on. Ajicic is at one end of this extreme. Living in this community, you really don't have to speak Spanish, as you're surrounded mostly by other expats who probably come from a similar background. Many of the businesses in town are owned by expats as well.

Surrounding Villages

Riberas, San Antonio and Mirasol are 3 areas to note between Chapala and Ajijic. Expats seem to like the small feel of these areas and can drive to nearby towns for shopping or entertainment.

Jocotepec is located on the west end of the lake. It's considered the industrial village. Although there are expats in this area, they tend to be in a housing area called Roca Azul. The malecon is very nice and larger than Ajijic, but a car is really needed if you live in this area and want to be involved in any kind of social activities. The village shuts down super early so you would need to drive into Ajijic or Chapala for any evening activities.

There are fewer English speaking locals as well. San Juan Cosula and Chantepec are 2 villages located between Ajijic and Jocotepec that boast several housing developments. San Juan Cosula has a racket club with rentals but the town is quite dead at night. Chantepec is a poorer village with some beautiful homes. Even so, it hasn't drawn many expats to the area.

Familia O'Grady 2014

There are definite pros and cons to each village, which is why it's important for you to know what 'must haves' are most important. If you're moving down with school aged children, the best schools are in Ajijic. Medical care is offered everywhere. You can be as busy or as leisurely as you wish. With the extra time in your day to feed the creative soul inside, you might consider attending one of the many artistic groups in the area. You can paint, quilt, sing, or play an instrument. Whatever life you're looking to create for yourself in Mexico, Lake Chapala has something to offer.

Puerto Vallarta

Puerto Vallarta is a magical city on the northern coast of Jalisco that has long been a favorite destination for expats. With a population of around 300,000 residents, about 20 percent of those are expats.

The city is a cosmopolitan enclave with old school colonial charm. Despite the infusion of expats from all over the world, everyone I spoke part the foreigners blend harmoniously with the laid back locals. If you're looking for a cosmopolitain beach paradise that is close to a major city (Guadalajara) and has its own international airport, Puerto Vallarta could be your pick!

The city is situated on the Bay of Banderas, one of the biggest bays in the world, molded to the contours of the Pacific Ocean. The setting is truly as beautiful an ocean destination as you'll find in the world. The city has an incredible artistic vibe, as it has become a haven for painters, sculptors and artisans from all over the world.

As you can imagine, there's a wide range of lifestyles available to expats. "Old town" Puerto Vallarta is an area where many of the locals live, as well as expats looking to integrate and save some money on expenses. Oceanfront property, both

with expressed for the most

renting or purchasing will cost you.

Just north of Puerto Vallarta is another town called Nuevo Vallarta that is made up almost exclusively of expats who live in luxurious gated communities.

Acapulco

Acapulco used to be the number one vacation spot in Mexico. Bill and Hilary Clinton came here for their honeymoon. It's a pristine slice of coastline about 4 hours from Mexico City. It's home to luxurious resorts, posh nightclubs and white sand beaches. Unfortunately, in recent years Acapulco has seen a drastic rise in violent crime, presumably due to the redirection of drug trafficking routes, making it a battle ground between rival cartels. At the time of writing, it has the second highest homicide rate in the world, ranking after San

Pedro Sula in H Scary, I know.

Since the ri violence, Acapulco has seen a dramatic drop in tourism and foreign residencies. However, expats I spoke with in Acapulco told me that the violence, as awful as it is, doesn't affect their every day lives because it's concentrated exclusively in the outlying, working class neighborhoods that are hotspots for gang activity.

Oaxaca

There's a famous song by Oaxacan singer Laila Downs called "Cumbia de Mole" that begins with the lines,

"They say in Oaxaca, they drink coffee with mezcal.

They say that the herbs can cure wickedness.

I like the mole that Soledad is going to grind for me

dear Soledad, is going to ᴐook a molito for me

Under the skies of Monte Alban

At night I dream about you"

The lyrics flow much better in Spanish, but this song really epitomizes the magical, fun-loving vibe that makes Oaxaca such a special place. The state is most well known for its one-of-a-kind gastronomy. The food and

drink in Oaxaca brings indulgence to a new level. Ask most Mexicans where the best of the best comes from and they will tell you Oaxaca. Mezcal, dozens of variations of Mole, the best chocolate in Mexico, it all comes from Oaxaca! Need I say more?

Oaxaca de Juarez, Oaxaca

The Capital of Oaxaca is ingeniously named after the state as so many are in Mexico (I wish someone had told Mexico's founding fathers that a little creativity goes a long way. I mean come on, it's super confusing!).

It's been a popular destination for expats since the 1970s. The city is pretty small as far as capitals go with a population of just over 260,000. This is one of my favorite cities in Mexico. If you're the kind of person that's looking for a vibrant, passionate culture to thrive and keep you on your toes, then Oaxaca is definitely your oasis.

Chiapas

If you're a nature lover who can't quite make up your mind what kind of natural paradise you prefer, Chiapas could be the place for you. Mountains, jungles, beaches, bustling colonial towns, the Southern most state in Mexico has got it all.

San Cristobal de las Casas, Chiapas

This is the first place I visited in Mexico and it made an instant impression on me. I was working in Guatemala at the time and I made the 8 hour bus ride to renew my visa and spend a weekend in Mexico. I remember vividly sitting on the roof of my hostel, scanning the horizon, gazing out at the stucco thatched roofs, rolling mountains, and colorful church steeples, thinking about what an amazing place this was.

I spent two full days wandering around the labyrinth of cobblestone streets, hidden markets, sprawling walkways and eccentrically colored buildings and churches. At the time I had no idea I would be coming back to Mexico to live, but San Cristobal definitely made a hell of a first impression.

As I mentioned briefly in the historical section, the city is also the site of one of the most significant revolutionary resistances in Mexico's history. Now twenty years after the indigenous Zapatista army descended from the mountains and stormed the city of San Cristobal, demanding equal rights and an end to oppression, the revolutionary spirit remains strong in the city.

A small colonial city of about 170,000 inhabitants, San Cristobal is a primary destination for expats looking for a laid-back lifestyle, mountain setting and autumn-like weather. Although the expat population here is relatively small compared to places like Puerto Vallarta, Lake Chapala or San Miguel de Allende, the city's rich culture and extremely affordable living prices make it an attractive alternative. For example, renting an apartment in San Cristobal will cost you about half of what it will in

any of the aforementioned places.

Non-Profit Central

For young expats looking to get involved with community development work, or retirees who want to get involved, San Cristobal is the place to be. The mountain region surrounding the city is unfortunately home to some of the poorest communities in all of Mexico. Dozens of national and international organizations have sprung up in recent years to attend to those needs and they employ expats from all over the world who make their home in San Cristobal.

San Cristobal is an ideal destination for a nature lover who doesn't need a big city, but likes to socialize and doesn't want to be off the beaten track. The streets of San Cristobal are safe and easily walkable. If you're like me and get a bit grumpy in oppressive heat and humidity, then the fall-like weather in San Cris might be perfect for you.

Palenque, Chiapas

Mexico is full of shocking geographical contrasts, but the difference between San Cristobal and Palenque definitely takes the cake. Just a mere 136 miles apart, the drive between these two cities will take you from the airy mountains to the heat of the tropical jungle. Palenque receives hundreds of thousands of tourists and travelers who come for the ecotourism and one of Mexico's most famous archaeological zones.

Mexico has hundreds of ruins and pyramids throughout the country, but the site in Palenque is the most magnificent. Hidden in an expansive natural reserve in the middle of the jungle, a trip to the pyramid site is easily an all day affair. Being in the presence of so much history is a humbling experience.

Palenque is an incredible place to visit, but frankly, I wouldn't recommend living there unless you're accustomed to oppressive heat and humidity, or you have a bit of a Tarzan fantasy and have always wanted to live in the jungle. But then again, this is coming from a Massachusetts boy with pasty Irish skin. The city gets thousands of tourists a year, but just a handful of expats end up staying. Those who do fall in love with the jungle mystique and never leave. These resilient expats are rewarded with pyramid sites, numerous waterfalls, and access to jungle hikes.

San Miguel de Allende

Since the 1970s, San Miguel de Allende has been one of the most popular destinations for American and Canadian retirees. Over the years, it's experienced plenty of ups and downs. Its "gringo-fication" threatened to turn every taco stand into a yoga studio, but I found it to be a remarkably beautiful, charming Mexican town that happens to be home to numerous expats. Depending on what time of year you visit, there are anywhere from 10,000 to 15,000 foreign residents living in San Miguel, making up about 10 percent of the population.

If you're an artist or art enthusiast, the streets of San Miguel will speak to you. Despite the influx of outsiders, the town has a remarkably distinct, romantic feel that entices you.

Every block in downtown San Miguel has either an art gallery, restaurant/bar or boutique hotel, and sometimes all of the above. It certainly carters to the hundreds of thousands of visitors that flock to the city. There are frequent festivals, parades, and cultural events, celebrating traditional Mexican holidays as well as art and film festivals. It's a city that oozes culture and at the same time offers the comfortable amenities of home in a Mexican colonial setting.

Personally, when living abroad, I love being the only, or one of the few gringos in a local community. If this is one of your enticing exotic thoughts about living abroad, you probably won't feel comfortable in San Miguel. Even though expats make up only 10% of the population, they have a dominating and sometimes overwhelming presence.

You will be less forced to adjust to a new language and culture in the same way that you would living elsewhere in Mexico. The environment in San Miguel has certainly accommodated the expat community.

As with any expat destination, you must visit San Miguel to take in the vibe for yourself and decide if it's the kind of place where you want to settle

EXPAT EXPERIENCE

"I lived in San Miguel in the late 90's when it was mostly hippi painters. It used to be the kind of place where the disaffected would come to live. Then it got really gringofied for awhile, so much so that I actually moved out, I wanted to live in real Mexico. Now it seems like all of the original hippies have had children and it's a much better place for families. I notice a lot of big, moderately priced apartments that cater to families. Although the prices might be higher here than in other parts of Mexico, it's a very affordable place to live if you have any kind of residual income. If you're a young parent, it's a great place to be. If you want a tradition school base, they have everything here, a Waldorf program and a bunch of Montessori programs. Many of these programs are for people with modest means to provide great bi-lingual education for children.

My number one piece of advice for people looking to move to Mexico would be that when you get here, make friends with locals! Aside from the moral, philosophical idea of being a good guest, the better your understanding of Mexican people and Mexican culture, the more enjoyable your life will be. It will open doors for you. You have to acknowledge that the locals have a particular way of life and they've been here longer than you have. I've learned to have faith in that living in San Miguel."

~ Mikko Machiato, New Orleans

down. Due to its central location, there is easy access to Mexico City, Guanajuato, Quetaro, and many other towns of interest.

You just might fall in love with the place like thousands of others before you.

Mikko Machiato, a writer from New Orleans, has been coming down to San Miguel and surrounding areas since the early 1990s and recently made the permanent move with his two young daughters. I caught up with him near the central square to talk about the evolution of San Miguel as a destination, what he loves about the place, and some advice for fellow expats considering the move.

t's worth, if I had my choice of any place to live in all of Mexico, I would choose Guanajuato. It's hands down one of the most magical cities I've ever been in. Most Mexican cities or towns follow a logical linear layout, with the central plaza in the middle of the town and streets and neighborhoods branching off the plaza in a grid-like manner. Guanajuato breaks all the rules with it's labrynth of impossibly narrow streets winding up steep inclines. The city is built in a valley and it appears that the mountains dictate how the streets were designed. Candy-colored houses and enormous domed cathedrals make a simple stroll through Guanajuato an eye-popping experience.

Guanajuato is just starting to gain interest as a go-to destination for expats. It doesn't have the notoriety of San Miguel or most of the other destinations mentioned for that matter, but it's every bit as beautiful and unique as any city in Mexico.

Everyone falls in love with a place for different reasons, not all of which always make a whole lot of sense. I fell in love with Guanajuato because of its completely ridiculous layout and its edgy yet charming character.

Guanajuato is first and foremost a college city. The University of Guanajuato is one of the biggest and most prestigious Universities in the country. It is also home to amazing museums, theaters, and a one-of-a-kind architectural style, nestled in-between a rolling mountain range.

Merida

In recent years, Merida has burst onto the scene and established itself as a viable expat destination.

The capital of the Yucatan state sets itself apart with its tropical climate, vibrant cultural and modern big-city amenities. The city is only about a half hour away from the beach and offers a wide range of affordable housing options, from deluxe gated apartment complexes to 200-year old colonial mansions.

Vicky Hillman moved to Merida in 2009 from Vancouver, B.C. and immediately fell in love with the tropical climate and unique colonial architecture. She was looking for a place where she could work or start a business to sustain herself and was able to land a job teaching English to the employees of an international company that has its headquarters in Merida.

She now runs a business that helps new expats settle into Merida, assisting them with everything from finding a place to live, immigration, vehicle registration and langu.. classes.

EXPAT EXPERIENCE

"Merida is a real hotspot right now. There are over 6,000 expats living in the area, some of them closer to the beach by El Progresso. There are plenty of bi-lingual schools and I've noticed more and more families are relocating with their children. I've met a lot of young couples that come to live here because they can work from home. Whether you want to kick back and relax in retirement or throw yourself at the local culture, Merida is a great place to call home.

My advice would be not to get caught up in the romanticism of owning a huge colonial house if you don't need it. Rent before you buy so you can give yourself a chance to get accustomed to the city, especially the heat, which can be pretty intense in May and June."

~ Vicky Hillman, expat from Vancouver, B.C.

For more information and advice on life in Merida, you can contact Vicki at Merida Expat Services, iteach@live.ca.

s another beau... al city that has always managed to fly under the radar, for both expats and travelers. If you're looking for a city with colonial architecture and waterfront properties, Campeche is definitely worth a look.

There is a boardwalk that lines the water for miles. The history is evident by the cannons that line said boardwalk. While the stroll has historical significance it's also up to date with separate lanes for walkers, runners, and bikers. The 275,000 folks are laid back and enjoy the colonial vibe.

There are plenty of markets, festivals, and a thriving night life. Plus, it's close enough to use as a base camp when exploring Mayan cities.

If you're a fisherman/woman or just like to enjoy the fresh catch, the region is home to tarpon, snooks, and barracuda.

Overall, it's a great solution for people who are looking to blend big city amenities with a flavor-filled colonial vibe.

Tulum

Tulum is best known for its magnificent beachside Mayan ruins that attract hundreds of thousands of visitors each year. As a long-term destination, it offers a refreshing, laid-back alternative to the glitz and glam of Americanized Cancun or Playa del Carmen. The three-block downtown area is lined with seafood restaurants, quaint cafés and gelato bars, hostels and way too many scuba schools. The road to the beach is where you'll find all of the boutique hotels, cabanas, spas and a handful of luxury apartment complexes.

Right now, Tulum is more of a backpacker haven than expat hub. However, when I was there I did see a beachside apartment complex or two under construction. I visited a one-bedroom apartment with a small pool and Jacuzzi that was renting for $400 a month, utilities included. Not bad for a Caribbean beach town. Oh yeah, I should mention that the road to the beach is lined with a beautiful bicycle path, so don't worry if you don't have a car.

Every slice of pristine beach in Tulum is something off a postcard, without tacky skyscraper hotels polluting the view.

Akumal

Between Tulum and Playa del Carmen lies the sweltering beachside community of Akumal. Impressively designed mansions line the road that leads to Akumal's private beach. At the time of writing, Akumal was experiencing a lot of growth for a town its size. I saw a handful of construction crews building new homes and complexes.

The downtown area of Akumal, if you can call it that, is at the entrance of the highway and boasts a handful of quality restaurants and a well-stocked general store. The public beach is the best place in the area to swim with sea turtles. There's also a small marina where local residents dock their boats.

Akumal could be an ideal destination for you if you're looking for peaceful, relatively affordable beachfront property.

Cancun

Cancun is one of the most popular beach destinations in the world, attracting hundreds of thousands of tourists each year. It has miles of beaches and all-inclusive resorts, packed to the gills with sunburnt American tourists enjoying a boozy vacation. Driving through the city packed with car dealerships and shopping malls, you could easily forget you were in Mexico.

You've probably got the impression right now that I don't have the highest opinion of the place. The truth is, it's a lovely place to visit and enjoy a vacation but I haven't met anyone who has chosen to live there. It doesn't feel Mexican. There are dozens of alternatives if you're looking for a slice of beach paradise that exude a Mexican flavor.

Islas Mujeres

Do you every dream about living on a tiny Caribbean island? Islas Mujeres is a 30 minute ferry ride from Cancun but a world apart from the abrasive skyline of Cancun's resorts. The entire island is only five miles long. In recent years, there has been a development boom and lots of relatively affordable waterfront property has gone on the market and been snatched up by expats.

To get there, take the ferry from Cancun's Puerto Juarez. Upon docking at Isla Mujeres, try renting a golf cart or a scooter to explore the island. It's a great way (really the only way) to get off the beaten track and see the entire island. Many of the hotels will offer discounted rates for extended stays during the low season.

Baja California

Baja California, or lower California, is an 800 mile long peninsula that separates Mexico's mainland from the Sea of Cortez. The peninsula stretches over 1,000 miles between the Pacific Ocean to the west and the Sea of Cortez to the east, which famous French oceanographer Jacques Cousteau observed as "the aquarium of the world."

The peninsula is comprised of two Mexican states, Baja California (Norte), with Mexicali as capital, and Baja California Sur, whose capital city is La Paz. Because of its proximity to the U.S., the state has long been one of the most popular destinations for American retirees.

The northern most sections of the states offer an easy drive from major cities in southern California like Los Angeles and San Diego. Some residents who live in the northernmost cities of Baja California Norte are able to live in Mexico and commute to work a few days a week in San Diego! The border traffic can get a bit intense at times, however, so be prepared for a wait.

The peninsula is packed with popular destinations for day-trippers, vacationers, and thousands of expats who make their home just a short drive from the U.S. border.

Until the early 1970s, Baja California Sur had a population density of less than one inhabitant per square kilometer! It has since picked up slightly, but things haven't changed radically, so you'll find plenty of crowd-free spaces and isolated beaches.

This is a great place to be if you love water sports, fishing and want to be within driving distance to the U.S. However, living costs here are significantly higher. I'd recommend living no closer than 20 minutes to the border to avoid the congestion and border vibe (which can tend to be dingy).

Ensenada

In the past 20 years or so, Ensenada has grown from a small fishing village, to a bustling city of about 200,000 residents, about 15,000 of whom are American expats. It's only about a two-hour drive from San Diego and some expats who live in Ensenada cross the border on their daily commute to jobs in San Diego. It's especially popular among fishing and sailing enthusiasts, who can dock in Ensenada's marina and come to the mainland to enjoy the city's colorful restaurants, lively nightlife and traditional Mexican flavor.

"I loved driving with friends for a day trip to Ensenada for affordable and delicious Coronas and Lobster dinners." Shannon Enete, San Diego

La Paz

If you're looking for a costal port-city with a tranquil, provincial atmosphere, La Paz is definitely worth a visit. For the ocean lover, La Paz overs a refreshing alternative to the upscale resort feel of Cabo San Lucas. It wins on setting alone, surrounded by both ocean and barren desert. You can go surfing, fishing and

moto-crossing on sand dunes in the same day!

The population of La Paz hovers around 150,000, with about 5,000 full-time expat residents and perhaps more snowbirds who make the incredibly wise decision to spend their winters here.

As far as port cities go, it's tough to beat La Paz. Breathtaking seaside views, beaches, wildlife, plentiful delicious seafood, moderate living costs and access to modern amenities. It also has one of the lowest crime rates in all of Mexico and the highest standard of living in terms of per capita income.

San Jose del Cabo & Cabo San Lucas

San Jose del Cabo is the more laid-back and less fancy sister city of Cabo San Lucas. It's more a lar many expats. It's just 20 miles form the resort of Cabo San Lucas with its busy marinas and high energy vibe.

Along with Cabo San Lucas, this really is the playground for the wealthy.

Luxurious gated communities and country clubs line the coast-line. If you've got the dough, this is without a doubt a beautiful place to be. The beaches set themselves apart from other costal locations in Mexico with mind-altering red rock formations lining the beach in the middle of the sea!

As beautiful as they are, any effort at a traditional slice of Mexico feels somewhat forced and pandering to the hundreds of thousands of tourists that flock to the beaches every year. Outside of these cities, there are plenty of small towns and popular RV camping sites for the outdoor adventurer in you.

Loreto

Desert and sea unite in Loreto, one of the oldest settlements on the Baja peninsula. Its beautifully preserved history is on display with 300 year-old churches and missions lining the boardwalk and central plaza. In Loreto you will find tranquil beaches and the turquoise waters of the sea of Cortez, without the crowds at other more popular destinations along the coast.

Loreto is a viable destination to settle down and find your slice of paradise on the Baja peninsula. The city is rich in culture with music, art exhibitions, concerts and festivals giving a colorful vibe to the city's streets.

Todos Santos

Just over an hour away from Cabo San Lucas, this "pueblo magico" is experiencing a renaissance as more and more tourists and expats discover the casual, rustic atmosphere that permeates life in Todos Santos. It's known for its cool climate, with temperatures in the mid 70's year round. Although real estate prices are climbing steadily with its increased popularity, Todos Santos is still a bargain compared to the resort destinations further down the coast. Here you'll find the infectious charm of small town Mexico. In a few years, the secret could get out and potentially drive up prices and crowding on the now pristine and relatively deserted beaches.

«RENTING VS. BUYING»

RENT

There is no denying my bias towards renting. The benefits are numerous and include:

Flexibility: Depending on where you are and what kind of apartment you are looking for, many landlords will allow you to rent on a month-to-month basis, saving you the trouble of signing a contract and having to commit to a fixed period of time.

Simplicity: It's relatively easy to find an apartment or a room, with services included, saving you the trouble of having to pay your electricity and internet bills every month.

If you decide after a couple of months that you don't like your neighborhood, apartment, or community, then you can just up and leave and try somewhere new.

Maintenance: If something breaks in the apartment, such as the fridge or the air conditioner, you don't have to worry about footing the bill for a new one.

You can allocate a higher percentage of your income to travel, sampling the many beautiful destinations and trying them on for size.

The perks of buying include:

That sought after stability

Lower monthly costs if you plan on staying long-term

If you opt to rent make sure and ask the following questions:

What does your rental rate include (homeowner fee, water, electric, tv cable, gas)?

Ask for an inventory list. Don't assume that just because your condo doesn't have a coffee maker you'll be supplied with one. Each unit is as is unless specified otherwise. If you don't like something about the unit, negotiate changes before you sign.

Another common myth is if you decide to spend money on your own accord to "improve" the condo, don't assume you will be reimbursed. Also, if you break your rental lease for whatever reason (even a death in the family), you lose your security deposit.

BUY

Just because I am clearly pro-renting before buying does not mean buying is without benefit:

Homeowner benefits include:

Continuity

The freedom to create your customized oasis, the dream home you always wanted

Potential path for immigration (see the Immigration section)

You have potential rental income

You don't throw away money on rent (something that doesn't contribute towards ownership)

You can personalize the heck out of your house

A chance to gain equity if the value rises, which if you're in it for the long haul, is very likely to happen

Often, a lower monthly housing expense, that is fixed and could be paid off over time.

«COST OF LIVING»

How to design a budget to fit your lifestyle, cut your costs, and get the most punch for your Peso!

Mexico is unique in that most destinations have a surprising broad spectrum of living expenses, depending on your lifestyle. Day-to-day expenses, such as food, rent, eating out, and entertainment, are significantly cheaper than they would be in the U.S., Europe or Canada. However, luxury items like electronics, computers, clothes and shoes, can be surprisingly expensive. Overall, Mexico is a bargain no matter where you are coming from. Most expats that I spoke with told me their living expenses are anywhere between 25 to 50 percent of what they were back home.

I live in Mexico City, which aside from tourist hot-spots like Cancun and Puerto Vallarta is probably the most expensive place in the country to live. Still, I have been making slightly less than $1,000 a month and with that have been living comfortably, eating well, and traveling occasionally. As a single twenty-five year old, my living expenses might not be comparable to those of an expat couple, but it can certainly give you an idea of your options.

I rent a room in a large apartment.

My monthly expenses:

Rent & Utilities: $350

Cell phone: $40

Groceries: $120

Transportation: $25

Entertainment & Eating Out: $200

Grand Total: $735 USD

I'm pretty nomadic so I don't spend much money on clothes or housing fixtures. I try to buy all my groceries at the local market, which is significantly cheaper than shopping at the supermarket. I tend to go on a weekend trip at least once a month, so my entertainment costs could be higher than yours would be if you keep to yourself and stay at home.

HOUSING

There is such a range of housing prices in Mexico, it's useless providing one. I recommend you make a list of priorities to nail down what you can't live with, and what you can't live without, helping you zero in on a price range. While housing prices for both renting and buying vary greatly depending on where you're looking to settle, there are certain universal truths you can count on:

Tourist/expat hot spots will always be more

expensive than areas off the beaten path.

For colonial towns, the closer to the Zocolo (or center of town), the higher the rent.

In beach locations, property costs tend to fluctuate with proximity to the ocean (captain obvious)

If possible, always try to go through a local realtor rather than a foreigner who has set up shop in the local market. I've spoke to multiple expats who have told me that prices are always lower with local realty companies.

«BEFORE YOU ARRIVE»

Moving is incredibly stressful. In order to minimize the stress, cost, and errors, organization is essential. While I don't mean to belittle large domestic moves, you will have new obstacles like customs, passports, visas, immigration paperwork, and language barriers! This will be your first big test in flexibility, the most critical attribute (in my opinion) in order to have a successful experience overseas.

Not to worry, hundreds of people have successfully moved to Mexico before you. We've gathered all of their tips, and learned from their mistakes to bring you the following pages. Keep an eye out for checklists throughout the section.

SQUARE UP DEBTS

Living in Mexico is infinitely more possible and manageable without debt. The heaviest anvils weighing you down are your credit card, car payment, mortgage, and school loans (if applicable).

Create a new budget and ditch as many "wants" as you can, leaving only your needs. If you have decided to embark on a life abroad then that is now your biggest *want*, so keep that in mind when you sacrifice small things like HBO or cable. In addition to ditching cable, start brown-bagging again and watch the savings pile up.

How to Retire Happy [2] by Stan Hinden delves deeper into ways to convert debt into retirement savings.

SECURE DOCUMENTS

Make certain you have secured all the paperwork needed before your departure. This will save months of frustration and hundreds of dollars. Read the Immigration section to learn how to get started on your paperwork.

If your driver's license or passport are going to expire soon, renew them now so they arrive before you depart! If you have children, make certain their passports and visa documentation are in order before your departure.

FOUR-LEGGED FRIENDS

Shipping your pets abroad has become fairly simple. More and more people are traveling and moving with their pets. Mexico is a pet friendly country with no breed restrictions and once your pet is accepted into the country no further heath requirements are made. You can travel with your pet from state to state without further paperwork.

---

[2] http://bit.ly/retirehappy

The Mexican government[3] has laid out the process very simply.

Get a Health Certificate (original or copy) issued by a private or official Medical Veterinarian indicating these 4 things (to be printed on letterhead with the license number or a photocopy of the medical license).

Name & address of exporter and importer (address of origin and destination address in Mexico)

Vaccinated against rabies (indicating the date of application and expiration date of vaccine), Pets under 3 months of age are exempt

Inspection found the animal to be clinically healthy

Name, signature, and license number of the Medical Veterinarian

issuing the Health Certificate.

Your pet needs to arrive in a kennel or carrier that is clean, without bedding, cloth material, or accessories

You may bring a day's worth of dried dog food or an unopened bag of food labeled in English or Spanish stamped by the food inspection authority (a total of 20KG per family is allowed).

If your pet is sent in cargo, it's important that you verify all requirements of the airline and consider the use of a customs broker to clear customs.

The above requirements are per the Mexican Government:

http://bit.ly/12liDn1

---

[3] http://bit.ly/12liDn1 Government site that spells out the pet import process

Pet Logistics

Microchipping dogs and cats has become a regular practice and is highly recommended. A microchip is a surefire way to prove ownership and is required for some pet transporter companies.

Once you have gathered your paperwork and have chipped your pets, you can shop for the best transportation for them. Make sure you're well versed in your airline's pet transport policy before you purchase your tickets. Some airlines restrict weight limits for in-cabin pets. Other restrictions often include maximum and minimum outdoor temperatures, nonstop flight requirement, and / or breed restrictions.

A good starting point would be to review the pet policies of the airline. A few major airline Pet Policies can be found below.

PET POLICIES

United:

http://bit.ly/unitedpetpolicy

American:

http://bit.ly/americanpetpolicy

Delta:

http://bit.ly/deltapetpolicy

US Airways:

http://bit.ly/USairwayspetpolicy

LAN:

http://bit.ly/LANpetpolicy

TACA:

http://bit.ly/tacapetpolicy

There are a few different routes you can go to get your loved four-legger to your new home. With many airlines, you can carry your smaller pets on board in a pet carrier for a fee. If your pet is a service dog, the fee is waived, and the pet does not need a carrier.

I recognize that there is a current trend where people fraudulently present their dogs as service dogs. While I am an avid dog lover, I worry this will take away rights from the disabled.

Make sure you read the airline's policy (the included links) and not a third party's site. There are numerous out-of-date sources of information in cyber-land. The last thing any pet owner wants is to show up for their flight and learn they can't bring their four-legged baby.

If your pet is not a service dog, nor do they fit under the seat in a carrier, then your options are restricted to shipping them as checked luggage or hiring a pet transporter.

Pet transportation companies are the second best option to riding in the cabin with you. They utilize smaller planes that are o\ temperature regulated. First-class pet transporters even include a vet tech or other caretaker to monitor your furry children, assuring their comfort.

Services like Pet Movers are pricey but will actually deliver your pet door to door! They also provide you with a moving counselor who will help facilitate the best schedule and route so your pet has the fewest connections possible. Moreover, they provide the kennels used during transit, the kenneling when necessary for customs, shots and paperwork as needed, and obtain international import permits! They're also a member of the IPATA and USDA pet handlers http://bit.ly/petmovers

Shop around and find the best pet transporter that fits your budget and requirements. There are many scammers in the pet transportation sector. I recommend visiting www.ipata.org to shop for your transporter. Only reputable pet transporters are awarded certification through the International Pet and Animal Transportation Association (IPATA). The website also includes information about insurance, vets, animal handlers and more!

MAIL SYSTEM

You need to reshape your mail to suit your international living.

Make sure you unsubscribe from magazines, catalogs, and other snail mail subscriptions.

Start a list of people and companies that you need to inform about your move. You'd be surprised how long the list grows over a few weeks.

Set up online billing and electronic statements for your bank, credit cards, student loans, etc.

Sign up for an absentee ballot if you are interested in keeping up with your rights in your home country.

If you have a family member or friend that's extremely supportive and wants to lend a hand, ask them to use their address as your base address and have them email you pictures of your mail as it arrives. If you've done your job well, this shouldn't be too many pieces of mail. This is a pretty big favor so I recommend occasionally shipping their favorite sweets via Amazon to them as a thank you!

Or invest in a mail service like US Global Mail, Becoming an Expat's preferred mail solution. They will provide you with a US address, scan pictures of your mail, and allow you to respond via a smartphone app with options to trash or ship your mail to you. Plans start at just $10 per month for individuals.

BANKING

Does your bank serve you internationally? Your local credit union or large chain bank might have served you well in your hometown, but as an international bank does it fall short? Evaluate your bank with the following criteria:

Can you fax a wire request to transfer money?

» Are there ATM fees and if so, are they excessive?

» Are there currency transaction fees?

» If you're receiving a pension, Social Security, or annuity, can the payments be automatically deposited to your current bank?(www.ssa.gov/foreign/index.html)

» Do they offer mobile deposits? (the ability to take a picture of both sides of the check and deposit the check without ever sending it in)

» Are they FDIC insured?

» Is there a minimum balance requirement to avoid maintenance fees?

Most banks charge a foreign transaction fee (a percentage of your purchase) each time you swipe your debit or credit card in a currency other than that of your country of origin. For example, if your bank charges a 10% currency transaction fee (CTF) and you buy dinner for $35 USD, your currency transaction fee will be $3.50 USD! CTFs add up quickly, as do ATM fees.

I didn't think to change banks before I moved abroad. In just six months, I racked up $210.67 USD in fees just to access *my* money! I now proudly bank with Charles Schwab and pay zero fees (information to follow).

Many towns in Mexico are still cash driven. Some small towns don't even have a bank or ATM. That's the exception however, more often cities have at least one bank.

Check to see what your bank charges each time you access your money from an "out of network" ATM. It's almost always the rule that the bank whose ATM you are using will also apply a fee. You could be looking at anywhere between $5-10 USD plus your currency transaction fee just to use the ATM!

You might conclude that your bank won't serve you well as an international resource. I've banked with Bank of America, Washington Mutual, and most recently Wells Fargo. I was paying way too much to access my money internationally, so I did some research and found a bank that offers everything I was looking for: Charles Schwab's High Yield Investor's Checking Account. *(I do not receive any kickbacks from CS.)*

Take a look at the benefits:

» Zero maintenance fees

» Zero minimum balance requirement

» ZERO CURRENCY TRANSACTION FEES

» Free brokerage account

» Mobile deposits

» Online banking

» UNLIMITED ATM FEE REIMBURSEMENTS- not only do they not charge ATM fees of their own, they take it one step further and reimburse you for the ATM fees other banks charge you to access your money around the world!

The only other time I've heard of ATM fee reimbursement is through small credit unions.

Wells Fargo has an account that allows you to withdraw money twice a month without a foreign currency transaction fee (usual ATM fees will still apply). The kicker is, however, you have to maintain at least $25,000 in the account to avoid a steep monthly account maintenance fee.

CREDIT CARDS

Just mentioning credit cards causes palms to sweat and increases the heart rate for the folks who've fallen behind in the brutal credit arena. While this section might not suit everyone, for those people who can stay disciplined and organized you can reap some seriously amazing benefits by choosing the right credit card.

I recommend having at least two credit cards for emergencies if for nothing else. If you already have your favorite credit cards, make sure they don't expire anytime soon.

It seems like every time I travel, at least one of my cards gets turned off due to a fraud alert. Even when I diligently call the card company ahead and report my travel plans. Having your cards turned off can be detrimental, which is why I always have three cards. I maintain two credit cards and one debit card, and I *never* keep all three on my person. I prefer to keep one credit card at home or in the hotel safe, and the other on me. I only carry my ATM card when I need to use it, otherwise it's in the safe with the back up credit card. When I'm in transit, I keep my passport, credit card, and ATM card in my travel pouch (under my clothes), and the other credit card and a small stash of cash in my zipped pocket easily accessible.

Do your credit cards reward your cost of living spending? Do they serve you? I can book a one-way flight to Thailand for $15 and 40,000 points with United Airlines, or a one-way flight to Cusco from Oklahoma City for just $32 and 20,000 points all because I signed up for their Business Mileage Plus Explorer Preferred Card and was given 40,000 for spending $3,000 in the first three months. Now that is serving my needs just fine!

I also won't tolerate currency transaction fees. There are plenty of amazing cards that do not charge them. Since I travel internationally, I look for cards with rewards for airlines that go to the countries I plan to visit, i.e. American Airlines and United.

I currently use the *Chase Sapphire Preferred* card and the *Mileage Plus Explorer*. Both of these cards dump into the same frequent flier pool. The Sapphire card allows me to transfer my points 1:1 mile into United's Frequent Flier program. In order to score this slick heavy metal card, you must have decent credit.

Another option is the AAdvantage card offered through Citi Bank in conjunction with American Airlines. I've never enjoyed working with Citi, but I will say it's incredibly easy to redeem your miles anytime on flights around the world. I've flown no fewer than seven times with this card.

The longest flight was from Santiago, Chile to Kansas City, USA. I paid $80 in taxes and fuel surcharge and used 30,000 miles!

If you have to make a purchase, you might as well make it work for you. The reason I switched to United from American was because American required that either my origin or destination be in the United States. United doesn't have this requirement.

I will give it to American, however, because their change fees are almost half of United Airline's, and they are excellent for last second flying opportunities.

ALL OF YOUR CRAP

Our belongings can cause a great deal of stress if not dealt with correctly. The first three questions you must ask yourself are: What do I need to take with me? What, if any, select items do I want to ship?

Would it make more sense to buy new furnishings or send my house-full in a container? Take a mental inventory of everything in your house. Out of everything in your cupboards, closets, and drawers, how much of it do you actually use on a regular basis? Many people are "collectors" with big houses to fill. Just because you own it doesn't mean you need to ship it.

The hardest decision about moving your belongings is whether to sell or donate everything and start fresh, or rent a container and deal with the daunting task of satisfying customs requirements.

STARTING FRESH

A new life with new stuff. You won't have to wait for your belongings to arrive, or deal with the hassles of importing into a foreign country. Instead, you'll have an open-ended ticket to shop for cool new local furniture.

In essence, it's a major spring cleaning of your belongings. Plus, selling off your old stuff could provide a nice chunk of change to help with moving expenses.

If starting fresh is your route, allow a few weeks or months to sell or donate everything outside of what you pack in your suitcases. Conquer one room at a time, leaving the kitchen for last since you will be using kitchen items up until the move.

Consider items that may be difficult to find abroad. I'm 6'0" tall which is rare in Latin America. Besides curious stares, it translates to difficulty finding clothes and shoes that fit. Keep that in mind while packing.

Craigslist, eBay, and Facebook groups are great resources when slimming down your belongings.

If you're a gadget geek like me, make sure you have your electronic system set before your departure. Many cities in Mexico doesn't have the latest devices available for sale or if they do, the import fees drive up the cost dramatically. The larger cities like Mexico City and Guadalajara will have many of your favorite gadgets but once again, you will pay a bit more for them. It's better to be prepared than gamble with this one.

Every situation is different. While my situation doesn't make sense to hold onto many possessions, your situation may be drastically different, including kids, a house full of furniture, antiques, books that you want to reference, and other items you value and wish to keep.

If you're moving from the US you have a few options. You can start over, you can pack up your SUV/car/truck brimming full with your stuff and pets and make the exciting journey on the road, you can ship a container or you can ship your cargo via freight.

Since Mexico is so close to the US and reasonably close to Canada, there aren't many folks that opt to ship a container. Nevertheless, here is the information for your consideration.

CONTAINER

If you have the perfect furniture set (bedroom / living room), you don't have to part with it. Nor would you need to figure out where to buy furnishings in a new country with a language barrier.

If you choose to move forward with a container, make sure to purchase insurance for the contents. Also, research your moving company. Ask expats for referrals.

Take time to make this decision, it's a big one. If you decide on using a container, make sure you're

prepared to wait weeks and sometimes months for your belongings. The average timeframe is 4-8 weeks.

INTERNATIONAL MOVERS

Finding the right moving company is key for any major move. Your moving / shipping company can mean the difference from having all of your belongings seized to a seamless tax-free experience. I speak aggressively not to scare you but to share with you the level of seriousness customs enforce regarding imports.

To begin your research, you can use search aggregators like www.intlmovers.com and www.moverreviews.com. The first allows you to enter your origin and destination locations, and they find companies that service your new and old areas. This allows you to request numerous quotes at once.

The second website collects hundreds of reviews for the most popular movers. Compare your quotes to the reviews, BBB,[4] and www.movingscam.com before making a decision.

Ask for references from customers that have shipped to the country you're considering moving to and call them. Question the references about any damage and how the company managed those issues. Ask, *"Were the shippers on time and could you track your shipment throughout the process?"*

These websites are great for generalized moves. Since importing to any country requires specialty knowledge of said country, make sure to do the research to assure your company is well versed and experienced in these rules and regs.

T+F TRUCKLOAD

This mover[5] while not registered with the Better Business Bureau is rated B+[6]. They've only had one complaint over the last three years with BBB and it was filed as resolved. T+F Truckload specializes in Mexico trans-border door to door services.

YRC FREIGHT

YRC[7] is unique because it is the only carrier with on-site, bilingual representatives at border crossing points in Mexico. The company states that this helps expedite customs clearance. However, on BBB there are numerous YRC Freight companies with various addresses. I'm not sure if this is a franchise or not, what I am sure of is only one out of 7 or 8 ratings placed them at A.

[4] Better Business Bureau http://www.bbb.org/
[5] http://bit.ly/TFtruckload for more info
[6] BBB rating http://bit.ly/tftruckload
[7] http://bit.ly/YRCfreight for more info

Their top performer was their location in Hawaii, many of the other locations were giving failing grades. YRC is not accredited through the BBB.

ACV IMPORT & EXPORT

ACV has been written up in numerous Mexican blogs as an excellent option for shipping cars and household goods. They have offices and trucks in San Diego, offering a simple solution for those nearby. The company has been in operation since 2003. I couldn't find a rating with the BBB.

They promise that once your items arrive in San Diego they will deliver it to your door in Mexico in seven days or less.[8]

OCEAN STAR INTERNATIONAL, INC.

While this mover maintains an A rating with the BBB and has been mentioned in Mover Mag and USA Today as one of the best moderately priced movers in the States, I cannot conclude that they are without errors due to some hellish stories I've read from their customers.[9] The short of it was, the client was guaranteed a lowball rate, then after all of their worldly possessions were gathered and across the globe, Ocean Star doubled their fee and held the belongings for ransom. "Come get your stuff or pay up" was how they treated their customers.

[8] for a quote contact: http://bit.ly/acvmover

[9] Read the full experience: http://bit.ly/movescam

AMERIJET INTERNATIONAL

"5000# LBS. in 5 Lift Vans, 1000 CU. FT. Gross.

Amerijet is rated on BBB with an A- and has 30 years experience shipping to Mexico. Their website is very user friendly and it allows you to quote a move via ground, water, or air. They recently launched a <u>youtube</u> channel to display their services. They even specialize in shipping your pets.

For 2,000 pounds packaged in 25 boxes roughly 2'x2'x2,' Amerijet offers an initial quote of $4,518 USD to take those 2,000 pounds from Oklahoma City to Guadalajara Mexico

REINER OVERSEAS MOVERS

I have read good things about Reiner and they score the elusive A+ with BBB. I contacted them for a ballpark quote to ship from Oklahoma City to Puerto Vallarta, Mexico. Here was their response:

THIS RATE INCLUDES:

Packing materials, labor, loading, trucking to Laredo, customs clearance, delivery to your door with normal access, unpack, same day debris removal.

EXCLUDES:

Insurance (can add for a fee), without insurance our liability is $0.10 per LB. Rate excludes government inspections, duties, taxes, quarantine/fumigation (if any).

$7,000 Door-Door."

ROADTRIP

Or you could opt to do what the O'Grady family did and road-trip south with everything but the kitchen sink! They packed their Trooper, and metal boat full to the brim with their prized possessions for their family of four (including twin 8 year olds), their trusted dog, and drove from San Diego to Central Mexico. They paid about $35 in taxes at the border and then later on a second road-trip paid another $30+ fee to nationalize their car.

critical component of their move. It must be 100% accurate, ordered sequentially, thorough, and all boxes must be labeled correctly. Any discrepancy will delay your container.

Each day your shipment is delayed could incur a hefty storage fee. You can see how spending extra time to make sure the lists are completely accurate before you send the container is time well spent!

If you're planning on shipping goods you'll need to get familiar with the following documentation:

DOCUMENTATION

The most important part of your shipping process is: "pack list, pack list, pack list." Every person interviewed (professional exporter or expat) stressed the importance of the pack list, and how it was the

Bill of lading[10]

Commercial invoice[11]

Detail packing list

Certificate of Origin[12]

NAFTA Certificate of Origin (if applicable)

---

[10] read a great article about what should be on your bill of lading document http://bit.ly/billoflading

[11] an explanation http://bit.ly/invoicec
[12] http://bit.ly/certoforigin for more information

ISPM15/IPPC mark for any solid wood packaging

AVOIDING SCAMMERS

The moving company:

» Should not ask for cash deposits before moving your items,

» Should have a physical address near your area, not a P.O. box,

» Should be licensed and insured,

» Should be a member of BBB (US side) and American Moving and Storage Association (AMSA),

» Should conduct an in-home evaluation for an accurate estimate, or require a detailed inventory list,

» Be wary of low-ball prices

See the end of this chapter for a moving checklist

SELLING YOUR CAR

Deciding whether to buy a car abroad can be tricky. The first time I moved internationally, I thought I would foot it everywhere. I'm apparently not as bad-ass as I thought. Within one week, I was looking on Craigslist for used beaters for sale.

You can easily sell your car a variety of ways: through Craigslist, the Autotrader, a used car dealer, or my favorite option, through Carmax. I have sold two cars to Carmax and really appreciate their quick and honest service. It was particularly helpful when my car was not fully paid off, because they made the process so simple.

I walked in and asked for a quote for them to buy my car. After about 25 minutes, their technicians had finished a review of my car and I was handed a printed guaranteed offer. I compared it to Kelly Blue Book, Autotrader, and Craigslist equivalents.

Sure, I would miss out on a few hundred bucks, but selling with Carmax was easy, convenient, and I could decide what day to give up my baby. So, I returned to Carmax the day before my flight, handed the sales team the guaranteed offer (good for one week) and asked to complete the sale. Twenty minutes later, I walked out the door with a check! *(I also really appreciate purchasing cars with them, but that doesn't apply here, just thought I would share.)*

I have also sold and bought with Craigslist and the Autotrader. But after using them all, I really prefer Carmax because I don't have to worry about the individual I'm going to meet (at my house or some public lot), and there isn't the awkward haggling process. That to me, in addition to the added convenience of keeping my car until just before I left, was worth the difference in price.

IMPORTING YOUR CAR

As of the writing of this guidebook, there is a temporary suspension of importation of ALL vehicles effective 9/1/14. The suspension is confusing for all and its duration is anyone's best guess. To make matters even more confusing, according to Mexican Customs (Aduana) it is illegal for a permanent resident of Mexico to drive a foreign plated car.

Local police in Mexico may tell you it's ok to drive a US plated car as long as you have a US driver's license, but that is only within their jurisdiction.

It's similar to the recent conflicts the US has seen with new state issued marijuana laws. It may be legal in California to buy pot with a medical marijuana license but because it's against federal law we've seen many of these legally operated dispensaries shut down by the Federal government via the DEA. While you may be told by the local police it's ok as far as they're concerned, it's the Federal authorities who are the ones who confiscate your vehicle. Driving a US plated car as a Mexican or full time resident can earn you penalties in the $3,000 range and jail time if the government deems the car's value at more than $10,000.

The moral of the story is to make sure you import the car legally and get Mexican plates!

Not all cars can be imported into Mexico. They practice ageism only allowing cars in between the ages of 5 and 30 years old for Baja and Baja California Sur. If you have a hobby classic car you can still import it but it will require more paperwork and permits. For the rest of Mexico, they require that the vehicle is at least 8 years old and only accept NAFTA (North American Free Trade Agreement) vehicles. You know your vehicle is a NAFTA vehicle if your VIN begins with 1,2,3,4, or 5.

Steps:

» Connect with a customs broker or freight forwarder (the international moving companies we already listed) who can give you a price for the the total cost to include the 16% sales tax (IVA) of the value of the car.

» Clearing customs with your vehicle. This process can take up to a week. I'd recommend you send your original title to the freight forwarder so they can clear it with customs. It can save you a week long wait at the border.

» Make copies of your government issued photo ID.

» Make payment of taxes and get a receipt (*factura*)

» Remove your license plate

» Wait until they notify you that your car is ready on the Mexican side

Once your car is in Mexico it will need to be insured. I recommend you plan ahead and get some bids from a variety of insurance companies that serve Mexico prior to this whole ordeal. That way when your on Mexican soil with your green sheets in hand (Pedimiento de Importacion) you can fax or email them to your favorite insurance and know what your costs are going to be ahead of time.

Make sure and try to get National plates. If you get Frontera plates they are only good for Baja California and Baja California Sur. If you drive a car with a Frontera plate in mainland Mexico you'll be in the same boat as if they had US plates. Which is why cars with National plates have higher value for resale.

Once you have the car in the location of your new home the you can register it. You can get temporary 30 day plates by showing your import papers to the nearest transito (traffic cops) office, which should buy you enough time to receive your plates.

To register the vehicle you need to pay your fees (tenencia) at Secrataria de Finanzas del Gobierno de

Estado. Then you'll get your car inspected back at the Transito office. In order to get your plates you will need to present proof of residence (utility bill), copies of your driver's license, your immigration documents (i.e. tourist card, residency card), the green sheets you got at the border and your receipt from payment at the border.

It really sound like a lot more work than it is. That being said, make sure you're in it for the long haul if you decided to import a vehicle because your car's title will be stamped with the date of exportation meaning in order to plate it again in the US or Canada, you will have to import it back. You can still take trips up north but you will have to make sure your insurance covers the required liability mandate in the US and Canada.

«ELECTRONICS & TECHY TIPS»

This section was designed to help you create your best electronic solution system, or said more simply, what gadgets you should take.

Some of you reading may think, "I'm moving to Mexico to get away from all of this." If that's you, feel free to skip this section. However, if you're hoping to find inexpensive or free ways to keep up with grandkids, nieces or nephews, or other loved ones, this techno stuff will come in handy.

If you are moving to an area serviced by a cable provider, it's a good idea to bring your own cable modem/wifi router.[13] This way you don't have to rent one from the cable company and can bring up-to-date hardware avoiding unnecessary slowing or glitches caused by older electronics. It can be tricky if DSL is still wildly used which requires a different type of modem, so make sure and check if there is cable service where you

---

[13] A good wifi/modem combo unit: http://bit.ly/modemwifi

plan to land. This is not a must have device, but is nice to have if you have the space to spare.

One gadget I recommend for any avid traveler or for those living in Mexico in a home constructed with cement walls is a booster[14]. With cement barriers your wifi signal, on average, won't reach beyond two rooms. I plug the booster in at the top of the stairs which then catches the wifi signal from my combo cable modem/wifi router and boosts the signal to the rest of the upper level. Since I'm on the verge of being a tech geek (I'm not savvy enough for the full title), I wanted to have access to the internet in each room of the house, and with my booster, waaa-laa, I have accomplished just that.

If you enjoy reading print books and magazines, the bad news is it will be more difficult to get your hands on English materials in certain towns in Mexico. There are a few book stores that cater to expats in larger cities and expat communities but don't count on it.

Electronic Readers are the most convenient solution. Sure, you can't smell the book or see how far you are by gauging the remaining thickness. You can, however, shop in the Nook, Kindle, and iBook store in addition to your library's free ebook download venue from the hammock in your villa, and instantly download your next reading pleasure.

I use a 15" Macbook Pro and an iPhone to run my businesses. I read on my ipad and my wife uses our Macbook Air. Yes, we're an Apple family. In addition to our computers I have a booster (mentioned earlier), an over the ear Beats headset (that I use everyday when I work), a

---

[14] A device that picks up the wireless signal and repeats it (increasing the strength)

http://bit.ly/boosteral

Yeti microphone for podcasts, and a Canon Rebel T5i for the video production side of my business. It's very likely that this bag of goodies is overkill for you, but if you're planning on owning a business you might consider some of these items.

OTHER ELECTRONICS:

» Laptop or Surface pro3

» iPad

» Up-to-date smartphone *(who knows when you will be able to buy a new one)*

» Mobile speakers[15]

» Apple Tv[16] or Chrome for Windows users.

» Waterproof case[17] for your phone (for those refreshing downpours on your beach walks).

» External hard drive[18] to back up all of the amazing photos you will take.

» *Power surge protector*- you can pick this up in Mexico but make sure you use it. Lightening strikes have literally blown up appliances here.

» *Thumb/Flash drive* to take documents from your computer to be printed at a *Copia* store.

» *Video camera and waterproof camera[19] with extra batteries (what good is a camera if the battery is dead?).*

» Nice pair of *headphones* with a mic for Skype.

» 140W adapter[20] for your car (plug in your

---

[15] Here is a link to an excellent waterproof bluetooth speaker: http://bit.ly/h2ospeakers
[16] a device that connects to your TV's HDMI input and allows you to sign into your Netflix and Hulu accounts, rent off of iTunes, and access and Apple computer music and video library right on your HD TV. Here is a link: http://bit.ly/appletv03

[17] The best waterproof case for iPhones is made by LifeProof: http://bit.ly/lfeprof
[18] An easy to use, speedy 1T back up drive is made by Lacie: http://bit.ly/lacie1T
[19] This video camera is best for rugged outdoor adventures: http://bit.ly/goproexpat
[20] This is the one I have: http://bit.ly/140Wadapter

computer, camera charger, heat pad, or other 120V items while you're on long road trips).

STREAMING MUSIC AND VIDEO

What to do, what to do... Movie nights can be great entertainers if you're not a night owl or in one of Mexico's many nightlife active cities.

If you're accustomed to Pandora, Hulu, Instant Movies on Amazon, or Crackle, I have good and bad news for you. At the time of my writing, they do not have many international licenses. The good news is you can download a free program to "bounce" your IP address. In laymen terms, the program will play hide-and-seek with the numbers that report to the internet

gods where the connection originates.

The program that I use is called Hotspot Shield.[21] There are numerous programs, but not all are free. You can listen to all the music you want. Another option for music streaming is Spotify which has less international restrictions.

Depending on your country, Netflix may work just fine with a slightly different directory of offerings than what you are accustomed to in the States. Since there isn't a DVD subscription available, they offer more instant-watch movies. While the catalog is larger, they take away some instant watches that are available in the United States. I'm guessing the variance relates to the show's copyright restrictions.

If you are a movie freak and would love to host movie night at your house or in your backyard consider getting a portable

---

[21] To review or download this free program go to: http://bit.ly/ipbouncer

screen and projector. Since it's dark so early, it would be a great way to spend some quality time with your neighbors!

BEST APPS FOR EXPATS

Jump into the app store and be immediately lost, intimidated, and frustrated. How do you find quality apps that will suit you? The best apps I've discovered have been mostly by word of mouth. As an expat who is a former Apple employee and a total Mac geek, let me share with you my favorite apps specifically with the expat in mind.

◆ **Skype**

Probably, the most used and most valuable app for expats. This is a must have app. So you have downloaded Skype on your computer. Once you have a

smartphone or tablet, download the free app and sign in.

I highly recommend making two purchases on Skype: an unlimited calling subscription (premium plan $60 a year) and a personalized phone number (another $60 a year). I purchased the subscription that allows unlimited calling to landlines and cell phones in the United States. I paid around $3 a month. Rates constantly change with different promos, but typically Skype rewards you for paying for the entire year in advance. The other purchase was just as important. If you don't purchase a number then businesses, family, and friends can't call you. While you can call them anytime you want, they will see a different number each time and not know it's you. You can choose your area code when you purchase a number.

I take Skype with me everywhere I can get cell

service on my iPhone app. That way, I can make a call to loved ones or for business back to the States. If anyone needs to reach me and I have Skype logged in on my phone, it will ring!

There are competing apps that offer similar phone service such as Vonage, magicJack, and TextPlus. Skype has been at it the longest, has a proven track record, and adds video conferencing and instant message features. The second most popular internet phone service is magicJack.

♦ Viber

Another free talk and text app that is growing in popularity, but unlike Skype it doesn't require invitation to connect to others. It automatically incorporates your phone book. The biggest drawback is those who you wish to communicate with must also be on Viber.

♦ WhatsApp

In case you have been under a rock for the last 5-7 years, texting is practically required to keep in touch with people. I'm certain you know people who refuse to answer their phone, but will quickly reply to a text. International text messages get pricey if you don't know about great apps like WhatsApp.

Build a free account and text away! The drawback is the person whom you wish to text needs to be a WhatsApp user. This, however, is an extremely common and well established app, so it shouldn't pose much of a problem. The app is also a great way to send pictures without getting charged fees!

An alternative app that doesn't require your text-ees to have the same app is TextPlus. With TextPlus, you can choose a phone number (including the area code), and that number will be your texting number. You can send and receive texts on said number for free!

♦ **Voxer**

"Breaker Breaker, Foxtrotter's on the move." I loved walkie-talkies as a kid. This app allows you to talk to other people just like you are both on walkie-talkies, or Nextels, except you aren't restricted to a 200 foot range. You can walkie-talkie with someone in Africa if they have the app and a cellular signal.

If you hate text messaging, you'll love this. If the second you get behind the wheel you need to text everyone, talk into the phone instead, and they will get your walkie message.

The downside of this app is the same as WhatsApp. The other user must also have the app downloaded, but they don't

have to be logged in to receive the message. The app will notify them a new message is waiting to be heard. In order to talk back and forth in real time, both parties need to have the app open.

♦ **Google Voice**

Google Voice allows the user to port their phone number to Google Voice and then forward it to a second number. Currently, they do not allow forwarding to an international number, but you can forward it to your Skype number!

It gets a little confusing, but basically you can tell Google Voice, via the set up on its website, which contacts you want to call and which of your phone numbers to use (i.e. the Skype number you purchased) then Google Voice will use wifi to make the call.

Other benefits include: multiple number call forwarding, a wide variety of voicemail options (different voicemail messages depending on the number dialed), an excellent spam call filtering, and voicemail transcripts via your email!

You must set up Google Voice from the States. It will not allow you to do so once on ground in Mexico. To learn more about how Skype and Google Voice can integrate see:

http://bit.ly/skypegv

♦ XE Currency

This app is exactly what it sounds like, a currency converter. Don't worry if you're too tired to figure out the math. Just enter the amount of Pesos in the app and see how much it is in your preferred currency.

♦ Google Translate

A translator app every expat should have in their arsenal is Google Translate. Even if you are not in the smartphone arena, make sure and take advantage of Google Translate on your computer. The biggest drawback of the app is that it requires cellular service or wifi to work. If you are struggling with the same word, however, it remembers previous translation requests.

♦ Word Lense

This app was recently acquired by Google. You open the app and click record on a sign you wish to translate. Word Lense instantly translates anything in print using your built-in video camera in real time!

♦ TripIt

As an avid traveler, I love this app! It's the ultimate travel organization resource. Sometimes I book my airfare, hotels/ hostels, and rental cars months out while other times only days ahead.

After I downloaded TripIt, created an account, and authorized it to access my email, I no longer needed to worry about printing or organizing my confirmation emails. I used to search my email for confirmation codes, reservation codes, etc. Now, because TripIt recognizes when I receive an email confirmation, it automatically adds the information to the app!

TripIt also allows you to create trips. I recently returned from a three month trip to South America. I was able to separate all of my reservations by creating multiple trips, each one defined by a span of dates: Machu Picchu trip, Ecuador trip, Wedding trip, and Honeymoon trip. It was so great to see all of my complex plans organized so clearly without an ounce of effort on my part.

After I set the dates, any new confirmations for those dates automatically got added to the corresponding trip. I was able to access my trip plans on my iPad, iPhone, or any computer by going to Tripit.com. How great is that?

♦ TripAdvisor

This app is great if you're on the move. My wife and I take last-minute road trips frequently, and TripAdvisor really helps us find hotels, attractions, and outdoor activities. I love the "near me" option. It's a great *save me* app when I don't do my homework! The downside is it's super slow. The lag factor is really annoying, but if you use it in a restaurant or hotel with wifi, it's not *as* bad as on 3 or 4G.

♦ **Convert Units**

This is really only needed if you are from the US. Since the United States is hell bent on being different, we don't know: what a price per kilo gets us, if we are speeding at 50 kph, how much space is 1000m^2, or how large is 2 hectares of land. Until you learn these new measurements, an app like Convert Units is very helpful.

♦ **Kindle**

Everyone has heard about the Kindle. What you might not have heard is how hard it is to find books written in English in Ecuador. Unless you are in Cuenca or other large expat community, it can be very difficult. So even though I prefer a book in my hand over a screen, I have completely sold out to the Kindle App. It's nice to have all my books in my skinny iPad and iPhone.

Kindle recently added *Kindle Unlimited* which offers unlimited reading for one monthly fee of $9.99. Interestingly enough, it was launched just a few short months after two other companies offered monthly subscriptions for unlimited reading.

I chose the Kindle App as my primary reader over iBooks and the Nook because as an Amazon derivative, it is often $2 or $3 cheaper than the Barnes N' Noble's Nook. All three programs have similar interfaces, so no deciding factor there. The Kindle has more inventory than any other book app. Even though I am a Mac geek, I don't see any Apple oohs and awwws like I usually do regarding their reader. I miss Steve Jobs...

♦ Overdrive

Use your library card and download free eBooks to *Overdrive* for your reading pleasure. Thousands of libraries use Overdrive, check to see if yours does. Why buy books when you can get them for free? If you don't have a library card, get one before you leave. All you need is a photo ID with a local address or an ID and a piece of mail with a local address. It's a no brainer! You will even have access to free magazines and newspapers.

♦ Oyster

If you read so much that the library offerings won't cut it and you would prefer a book over watching a movie on Netflix, then you may want to consider a subscription with the book version of Netflix, Oyster. With one monthly rate of $9.95, you can read unlimited books anytime, anywhere! They have a free trial, so check them out if it sounds up your alley.

♦ Dropbox / GoogleDrive/ OneDrive

Dropbox has been around the block many times now and is still the cloud service leader. There are numerous competitors these days: Onedrive, ShareFile, CX, Cloudme, TeamDrive, Egnyte, Huddle, Cubby, Syncplicity, Box, Amazon Cloud Drive, Wuala, SugarSync, and SpiderOak to name a few. I'm sure that many are just as good as Dropbox.

I am in the process of switching from Dropbox to GoogleDrive because I'm using Google everything, and GoogleDrive has a built-in feature in my email and chrome browser offering me added ease of use. The rumor is that OneDrive will be launching unlimited storage for everyone, which may tempt me to jump clouds again, but I'm not holding my breath.

A free subscription caps at 15 GB which is plenty for thousands of documents. I have many of my documents and manuscripts backed up for my publishing business on Dropbox. You can pay $9.99 a month for 1TB of cloud service with either GoogleDrive or Dropbox. I primarily use an external drive for my video production company, and a second external hard drive to back up my entire computer (including my pictures and video content).

Don't be caught without a backup in the States or abroad. You cannot recreate the memories captured in your thousands of pictures. I'm also sure you don't want to recreate that presentation for work or rebuild your music collection.

If you choose to land in the tropics, your computer liability increases. The humidity is like kryptonite to your hard drive, sand is the devil, and you can be sure that both will be in your computer if you live near the beach..

◆ Flickr

With Flickr, everyone is given 1TB for storage of photos for free. That's roughly 500,000 photos (the figure varies greatly depending on your resolution). You can even set it up to automatically save photos that you are taking on your smartphone instantly! Flickr can be used as an excellent online backup resource so you don't lose those priceless experiences so meticulously captured on camera! Plus you can easily share albums with friends via email or Facebook. Speaking of Facebook...

♦ Facebook

While you may not have been a "Facebooker" in the past, once you live in a different country you may re-think your stance. Facebook provides a way to stay connected and informed in your loved ones' lives. You can see pictures from their trips, watch their children grow up, and comment on each adorable photo, making a virtual appearance in their lives when a physical one isn't possible. You can also share your adventures in Mexico.

I know from experience that people love seeing new exotic places. After seeing some of your gorgeous photos, they might be compelled to plan a trip to visit you!

♦ Photocard

The post office system in Mexico is dreadfully slow.

Packages arriving empty is not uncommon. Postcards usually make it to the States but take 4-8 weeks! Photocard is a cool app that lets you assign a picture you have taken on your iPhone/iPad as the postcard cover, then allows you to write a message in a variety of fonts and sizes. It even has stickers so you can decorate the card. Once completed, you purchase one credit for $2.99 to have it printed and put into the US mail that day! Two to three days later, your grandkids, buddies, parents, or clients will be surprised with a fun, personal, and customized card from you!

♦ Weather Underground

I enjoy the interface of this weather app on the iPhone. One standout is it's hyper local specific reports. It utilizes social interaction to assure the accuracy from one neighborhood to the next. Other pluses: it's incredibly user friendly, gorgeous displays for forecasts, wind speed, precipitation, sunrise/sunset data, and has an easy to use radar feature. You can also easily add different cities around the world to the app so you can call up your family and ask them how the snowstorm is coming along.

◆ Google Maps / WAZE

Both of these apps are great GPS resources. I personally have utilized Google Maps as my primary routing app. There was only one instance living in Costa Rica where Google Maps didn't have the roads I needed to reach my destination (in this instance, Rio Celeste). Surprisingly enough, Mapquest did have the roads in question. My adventures in Mexico were 100% satisfied by Google Maps.

WAZE is a fun to use GPS app that also has social data

such as eyewitness accident information, police checkpoints, and more. It allows you as the user to add up-to-date information about an accident you passed, a broken down vehicle, or a cop with a radar gun locked and loaded! So if you're stuck in traffic, open up WAZE and see what the holdup is, or better yet, check WAZE before you commit to a route.

◆ Juice Defender Plus

Run this app to extend battery life on Andriod-operated smartphones. I could say something snide like, "Apple doesn't need an app like this because of their superiority," but now that would be rude!

«SETTING UP YOUR COMMUNICATION SYSTEM»

UNLOCK YOUR PHONE

Almost all phones purchased in North America are locked by their original carrier so only sim cards provided by the carrier will function with the phone. Make certain you can unlock the phone for use in Mexico. Otherwise, the phone is no good to you as an expat.

First determine if you're under contract with your service provider. If you are, you must either finish your term or pay a steep early cancellation fee. After your contract has expired or terminated and you have a zero balance on your account including your phone, you are legally entitled to an unlocked phone.

Each carrier handles the unlock differently. AT&T

has a customer service department that is "suppose to" unlock your phone after receiving a written request and the phone's IMEI number. I tried this route numerous times for my iPhone with no response. I found that using $10 and a third party service was the way to go. There are numerous services that do an excellent job providing you with a factory unlock (i.e. no hacking) within 24 hours. One that I have used successfully numerous times is:

http://bit.ly/unlckphone

T-Mobile's policy is if there is no balance remaining on the purchase of your phone, they will unlock it. Simply dial 611 which directs you to their customer service. Tell them you are going on a trip abroad and need the phone unlocked. It may take them up to 48 hours to complete the unlock.

If you have a phone with Verizon, Sprint, MetroPCS, Cricket, or U.S. Celluar, then it's time to go shopping because they are CDMA phones and will not work in most of Mexico. CNT has a very small network for CDMA service, but it's basically a joke. I believe it's best to just leave it behind in the States.

Mexico is in conjunction with the rest of the world on the GSM network. If this is all Greek to you, pretend that GSM is on one radio station and CDMA is on another but the dial is broken. The US decided to be different (shocker right?) opting for the CDMA network when it was new and exciting. So you can put your old phone next to your yardstick on your way out of the country.

BANDWIDTH

Make sure your phone supports the bandwidth that the country you're considering uses. You can go to www.phonearena.com and enter in your phone to find out which frequencies it supports.

SKYPE

Features:

» Skype to Skype calling

» International calls

» Call waiting

» Video

» Messaging

» Sharing

» Personalized number

» Smartphone app

If you are not already a Skype user then go to www.skype.com and create a new account. Take care to remember your user name so you can give it to your loved ones. After you create an account, make sure all of the people that you wish to "Skype" have also created accounts. Make a few trial runs to work out the bumps. Call up your mom, daughter, son, or BFF and ask them to login. Stay on the phone in case they encounter "technical difficulty." Test video conferencing, instant messaging, voice calls, and sending pictures or files over Skype. That way, when you're thousands of miles away, you will know how it works and the process required.

If you choose Skype as your main source of international communication, you will want to purchase a personalized phone number and subscription. See the *Communication* section in *After You Have Arrived* for more information.

TEXT MESSAGING

Texting has become a form of communication to keep in touch with our younger generation. In fact, there is a whole new language being created around texting. BRB... Ok, I'm back!

International texting gets pricey fast! There's a solution with a few excellent apps that allow you to text for free. *I use WhatsApp and TextPlus which I spoke about in* **Best Apps For Expats***.* Your Skype account will allow you to text but it will cost you. The amount is displayed in the lower right corner of the texting space. It usually ranges from 9-15 cents per message. You must add "Skype credit" before you can text.

MagicJack

» International calls

» Call waiting

» Transfer your number

» Use a regular phone!

» Smartphone app

» Caller ID

The most popular internet phone services are Skype and magicJack, hands down. If you prefer to use a wireless phone or even a wired phone at home, magicJack has some extraordinary gizmos so you don't have to take the call through your computer. Skype has come out with a few gadgets[22] recently to respond to the magicJack Plus.

MJ also has free call waiting! You are required to purchase the device that translates the cable-modem signal to a phone jack receiver. You will need a regular phone or computer to use the magicJack. You can either transfer your number or select a new one. They provide a 30 day free trial, but you are required to pay a subscription. If you decide to go with the magicJack, make sure and order the device before

---

[22] See some of the options ranging from $20-$100: http://bit.ly/skypephne

departure and bring a phone with you so you can take advantage of all the options.

DATA

Some people experience difficulty setting up their data services with their iPhone, iPad, or other smart device using international service providers.

APN settings are settings in your phone that occasionally need to be adjusted in order to assure your data plan functions correctly.

Once you have a sim card and are able to make calls, turn off the wifi and check to see if you can receive your email or search the web. If you can, then you don't need to make any adjustments to your APN settings. If you can't, then this is most likely the hurdle keeping you from connectivity. If you have no idea where the setting is located, Google "Where is the APN setting on a ___ phone?"

«Moving Checklist»

» Go to www.intlmovers.com and get quotes and companies that serve your two points of location

» Ask for recommendations from friends, expat forums, AREC, and read testimonials found in this chapter

» Double check with the BBB regarding the potential company

» Find out what the mover will do if an item is damaged in transit

» Obtain at least three estimates from various companies and compare their costs with their corresponding services and ratings

» Find out if the mover is registered with FMCSA.

» http://ai.fmcsa.dot.gov/hhg/Search.asp?ads=a

» Determine when and how your items will be picked up

» Acquire all contact information for the movers for each step of the process: before, during, and after the move

» Purchase insurance for your items

Moving Day

» If at all possible, be present to answer questions and oversee work

» Watch the inventory process and make sure the condition of your items is correctly documented because this list is used to calculate your taxes

» Keep your bill until you have all possessions in your new home and all claims are settled if applicable

» After the truck drives away, perform a final walk through so you don't forget anything

» Make sure the appropriate party has directions to your new home!

» If your contact info changes, update it with the movers and drivers

Delivery Day

» Be present to answer any questions, inventory the boxes, and direct traffic

» Supervise unloading and unpacking (if applicable) of your goods

» Make sure the inventory list reflects any damaged items before you sign any documents

» Pay your driver or sign documents authorizing payment according to the terms of your agreement

«After You Arrive»

You've arrived after you step off the plane, through the jetway, and out the doors where the warm moist air greets you, (along the coast) or the eternal spring zips across your face in Central Mexico.

"Bienvenido a Mexico"

Welcome to your new life as an expat. Make sure to soak up this moment, celebrate it! Don't rush past it, you are no longer in a hurry. Settle into the rhythm of the country you've chosen as your new home.

If you were unable to make an exploratory trip to check out each region and secure housing, make sure to plan for at least a few weeks of exploration, and hotel/hostel expenses while you find your rental. The last thing you want to do is jump into the first rental you see, since the region and your home will greatly affect your overall satisfaction with life in Mexico. The more places you tour, the better suited your selected home will be.

FINDING A RENTAL

Those of us from the US, Canada and Europe are often planners. We want to know exactly where we're going, how long we will be there, and exactly how much "there" will cost. This way of living doesn't completely jive with Mexico. The pace is much more relaxed here and isn't so internet centric. While it's possible to arrange your accommodations ahead of time and sign a lease for a year before you land, I highly discourage it. If you don't wish to spend the beginning of your trip looking at houses and regions then I suggest you take a separate "scouting" trip sometime before the actual move. Your best bet might just be to pick up a good old fashion newspaper and read the classifieds (in Spanish).

A scouting trip dedicated to hunting for rentals and exploring potential cities is a necessity! This is the best time to discover how close or far the grocery store is, and where the bus station or gas stations are. After you have viewed at least 8-10 homes, write down a list of must haves and wants to see which home suits you best. Assess the regions by using the system discussed in the *Where to Settle* section.

PURCHASING A HOME

If you haven't yet, read the *Renting vs. Buying* section before you proceed.

The first step is to gather referrals for an excellent attorney or broker making sure the referrals are from people who actually purchased property through him/her. Then set up an appointment and ask any and all questions you have about purchasing property after you have read this guide.

Next, start searching for properties in your desired location. If you opt to have an agent assist you, ask what their commission is upfront and get it in writing. That way if it ever changes for any circumstances, you have it in black and white.

Mexico doesn't have exclusive agent agreements, so feel free to shop around and see which agent you like the best, and who shows you properties that are closer to your wish list and budget.

PURCHASING A PROPERTY

If you have constructed a home in the United States then you are familiar with the seemingly endless details that are required in order to make a quality home. Add to that, minimal regulation, a language barrier, and a confusing permit process and you have a true international adventure! On the plus side,

labor is considerably cheaper than in the US or Canada.

Peruse listing at a slow pace. Consider potential growth, access to public utilities, and infrastructure. Remember, many of the owners of the properties you're drooling over are selling them because they made a hasty purchase. Do your research, and live in the area where you're considering buying prior to purchasing. Purchasing is a fairly quick process, selling can take years.

When house or property hunting, take into account you are in a new culture. Business is conducted differently in Mexico than in your home town. They prefer to do business in person and have a very strong Machismo tradition.

Don't shake a women's hand unless she holds it out first, instead bow slightly. Mexicans are close talkers, don't give any indication that their closeness is uncomfortable, it could be perceived as rude. Also, you might find handshakes, hugs, and other gestures linger longer than you're accustomed to. This is normal in the Mexican culture.

CLOSING COSTS & FEES

» 2% Acquisition / transfer tax (of the sale price)

» Appraisal Permit Fee (~.075% of the sale price)

» Public Registry Fee (.3% - .5% of the sale price)

» Certificate of no Liens or tax debt (Fixed fee ~ $95 and may vary)

» Bank Annual Fee (~ $500 per year for the bank to maintain the Trust, or *Fideicomiso*. The amount may vary)

» Notary fees (vary but must include drafting contracts, legal counseling, and obtaining the non-debt certificate called *non-encumbrance certificado*)."

The same person is usually responsible for calculating all of the taxes and will forward the payment to the government.

» Transaction Fee (~ $550 may vary)

» Escrow Fee will be charged if you choose to go through an escrow company instead of through your attorney. This account is usually initiated when you put down earnest money on a property (~ around $500).

INTERNATIONAL BANK LOANS

Most expats who arrive with the intention of buying, arrive with cold hard cash in order to secure their new abode. For those of us who have "eggless-nests," options are slowly creeping in our direction. If you buy directly from a new construction agent in an ongoing construction project, the construction company can often provide you with a financing option.

There are also people who have secured personal loans from their banks located in their country of origin. It can be a long-shot, but if you have a good history and relationship with a smaller bank, sometimes they will go to bat for you.

TIP

Consider which currency you want to purchase your home in. With drastic changes in one or the other, you could end up with a huge impact on your purchase price.

SQUATTERS

The last thing that any homeowner wants is a squatter in their house. In the United States, it's a health, safety, and financial hazard. In Mexico, Costa Rica, Ecuador and other countries that have squatter rights you're in danger of losing your property. *Listen up part-time expats!* Squatters can gain the rights to your digs!

If squatters occupy your "unoccupied" house and land and work for a period of time, they can accrue property rights. Eventually, they can apply for its expropriation from the "absentee landlord." There have been instances in rural towns on foreign-owned land where a large organized group of squatters entered the land and created make-shift shelters. Due to their size, it was much harder to evict them.

What do you do if you find out a squatter is on your property? You must immediately file for an eviction order. If you catch it early and you can prove it, the procedure could be simple. However, the powers that be tend to favor the squatters.

When purchasing a house, take extra care to make sure signs of squatters are not present. If there is a caretaker of the property, make sure they really are a caretaker and not a squatter that may already have rights to the same property you seek to purchase. If you are concerned about squatters, film your property frequently so you have proof of improvements and changes demonstrating the property is not abandoned.

If you plan to leave for an extended period, make sure you have a caretaker on the property to keep squatters out. You can place an ad in the "Caretaker Gazette" or other housesitting sites (listed in the *How to Live for Free* section) for someone to house or pet sit your property. You provide the chores to be completed daily and the time span they will reside on your property.

In exchange for taking care of your property, they receive a free place to live! It's a win win! Create a written contract that each party signs so that he/she cannot become a squatter. In addition, have a neighbor or close friend that you trust keep an eye on the property, popping in to say hi, and check out the place every few months.

LOCAL BANKING

To open a local account or not to open a local account, *that* is the question... There are pros and cons to establishing a local banking solution. Most expats opt to utilize a local bank for monthly bills such as cell phone, cable, groceries (ATM card), and rent. All things considered, opening an account opens doors for you.

Pros

» *Access to services*- You'll need a local account for many services. Some cell phone and internet providers require a bank account.

» *Replacement*-If you lose your bank card, it's easier to get replaced because it's in country.

» *Risk control*- Using your local card is also better for managing risk because you will never have large sums of money in said account.

» *Bill Pay*- You have many more bill pay options with local banks, which means less errands and less lines to wait in.

» *Street credit*- Drop that local card, yes, you are a local!

Cons

» *Hassle* - Initial hassles setting up the account

» *Risk*- Whatever money you have in the account is not FDIC insured and might not be as secure.

TYPES OF ACCOUNTS

There are three major account types offered in Mexico:

◆ **Peso Denominated Checking**

Minimum deposit from $500 - $1,000.

◆ **US Dollar Checking**

Minimum deposit from $500 - $1,000. The more expensive requirements are for accounts such as money market accounts.

♦ Certificates of Deposit

Minimum deposit $1,000 however the account is only offered in Pesos. This account is geared for the investor.

In addition to the these local account options the Mexican branches who offer offshore accounts have additional Money Market and CDs accounts for high earners.

Getting it Done

» The following paperwork will be required:

» Proof of address (domicile)

» Valid ID such as passport or driver's license

» For corporations, you'll need your Articles of Incorporation and Powers of Attorney

» If you want a dollar denominated account, you must be a citizen of the US or Canada

» Copies of everything

The two largest Mexican banks are Bancomer and Banamex, both can be found along the border and keep offices in the US and Canada.

LOCAL COMMUNICATION

♦ CELL PHONE

If you have a CDMA phone (Verizon, Sprint, UScell, or Cricket), it's no good in most of the world. It's best if you purchase a

GSM phone[23]. Don't forget to insure that it is unlocked and not under contract with a provider! *See more about unlocking your phone in the* **Before You Leave** *section.*

Take your passport, your unlocked GSM phone, and about $10 USD to a local wireless provider. The overall market leader is Telcel but ask around to find out which provider has the best coverage in your town. Purchase a new prepaid sim card, or with a residency card purchase the best suited package, and put the rest of the money on the account so you have some minutes available for use.

It's not as easy to keep your number on prepaid phones as it is in the US or Canada so if you change companies, you often can't port your number.

There are upwards of 10 cellular providers in Mexico but three major players dominate the scene: America Movil (a subsidary of Telmex, it's mobile market is served through Telcel), Movistar, and IUSACell. The last two are often cheaper than Telcel, but if you live in a remote area Telcel will likely provide the best coverage. Movistar is a close second. Check out their network coverage maps online and consult your neighbors to see which network is best for you.

If your town doesn't have internet providers, or you wish to have internet on the go with your laptop or other electronic device, you can purchase a 3G stick or hotspot device with one of the mentioned cellular providers.

INTERNATIONAL COMMUNICATION

Hopefully you've already set up your Skype account (or other provider

---

[23] GSM phones in laymen's terms are the phones that use sim cards

mentioned), subscribed to the best unlimited calling plan for your situation, and purchased a unique phone number where business connections and loved ones can reach you. If not, read **Communication Set Up** in the **Before You Arrive** *section.*

If you have a smartphone, launch Skype and make a test call in the app. Make sure to dial from the Skype app, otherwise you will use airtime and long distance fees will apply!

Confirm that everyone you want to contact has a Skype account and knows how to log in. For the technologically challenged, I highly recommend you assist them in setting up their Skype so you can test out the connection.

To add someone to your Skype contacts, click "Contacts" at the top of your screen, then "Add Contact," then key in either their Skype username if you have it, or the email that they used to set up the account. This procedure needs to occur on both sides before you can be seen online and available for chatting on Skype.

Download and install TextPlus on your smartphone as mentioned in the **Before You Arrive** section. Send a trial text message to a loved one and have them send one back. You are up and running!

Don't forget about FaceTime for those who have Apple products. You can either connect by using their cell phone number or their Apple ID email address. Each route is free utilizing wifi for the connection.

TRANSPORTATION

Your transportation solution can make or break your budget. If you're worried about your monthly overhead, one of the best things you can do for yourself is move to a place that is pedestrian and public transit friendly. Another cheap solution to this chronic problem is picking up a used scooter to manage day to day errands. They are cheap and gas efficient.

In addition to the purchase of the vehicle, you will have insurance, registration (safety inspection), maintenance, repairs, and fuel expenses to look forward to.

GATHER YOUR BEARINGS

"The most frustrating part about moving for me was I had no idea where to get anything. For example, I needed an extension cord, an aux cable, and an adapter to go from the old stereo in my condo to an aux cable input. I hadn't the faintest clue where to find any of these items. I also had no idea how to say "aux cable" in Spanish. My best shot was "hay un cable que usa para eschucar música en el carro?" Which is a really poor gringo way to say "is there a cable that you use for listening to music in the car?" See what I mean? Stuff that usually requires zero brain power suddenly gobbles up endless energy!

In San Diego, I would simply Google Map the nearest Target and be on my way. Not so much in other countries that aren't as "connected" as the US. Even if there was an obvious retail outlet for my wanted item, there isn't an online venue to search the location of the nearest store. Many stores don't register with Google, so they don't show up in a search. This is why your landlord, expat community, and local friends are priceless resources. They've already hunted down many of the items that you will need and want. If they haven't looked for it themselves, their buddy has and found it. Your network is gold! They will help answer:

- *Where is the grocery store?*

- *Where is the gas station?*

- *Where is a good mechanic? (referral)*

- *Where can you buy hardware items?*

- *Where can you buy furniture?*

- *How do I find a handyman?*

- *Where do I pay my water bill?*

- *Where can I recharge my cell phone?*

- *When in doubt, roll with the flow, wait and then wait some more."*

~ Shannon Enete

«ESTATE PLANNING»

Having your affairs in order is important no matter where you live. When you add the extra complication of an international residency, you need to take extra care in your arrangements for the unfortunate possibility of personal or spousal demise. Death is scary, horrible, and unavoidable... So we need to plan for it. We don't want to leave our grieving loved ones in a bind. That's the last thing anyone wants.

Consult an attorney from your home country to see how to organize your will to assure that your international residency won't complicate matters. If you purchase property, cars, or maintain bank accounts abroad, you should create a will for those international assets with an estate planning attorney in your international location.

Mexico has very traditional laws regarding your estate, but each state can vary. So make sure you find out if your state abides by the Civil Code of the

Federal District or has their own.

In Mexico, they don't have the "Right of Survivorship" like the US has allowing property to automatically transfer to the surviving spouse, instead the property owned 50/50 per couple will be pieced apart. The 50% of the estate will proceed the course deemed by Civil Code which begins with the children. If there are no children the estate follows to the parents, and if there aren't living children or parents then it falls on living siblings, then nieces and nephews.

There are ways around these government rules through trusts or *fideicomiso.* Speak with an attorney referred to you by a trusted source. There have been some nightmares on each side of the coin, having US assets held up because of Mexican domicile and having Mexican assets taken away from the surviving spouse.

Take care to include your burial or cremation wishes in the document. This decision is extremely personal, and in some circumstances religious. I will warn you, repatriating a body to your home country will cost you a fortune (if it's not covered by your insurance). Plus, it can be of a logistical challenge if the body is leaving the hot and humid coastal region.

CHECK LIST

» Make a budget to kill your debts.

» Assess your current bank and credit cards for international compatibility. Make changes as applicable.

» Obtain or renew passport(s).

» Renew driver's license if applicable.

» Gather immigration documents needed.

» Decide what to do with your stuff.

» If shipping a container, request at least three estimates from reputable movers.

» Decide which electronics you want to take with you and purchase the electronics that you need for the move.

» If you are a smartphone or tablet kinda' gal/guy, download and play with the best apps for expats.

» Make sure you have an unlocked GSM phone.

» Create a Skype account and share it with loved ones and business colleagues.

» Download a free text messaging app and try it out. Give your contacts your new texting number before you leave.

» Prep your car for sale, advertise and sell *(Carmax is a great option I have used twice).*

«FAMILY & EDUCATION»

Moving abroad with kids. Does it hinder or harm their future?

MOVING WITH A FAMILY

Uprooting your family in the pursuit of something better is a scary prospect. US citizens have been conditioned from a very young age that their homeland is the best and most sought after country in the world. The truth is, the best is not the same from one family to another. One country does not fit all.

I'm compelled to remind you there is nothing new about seeking social and economic opportunities elsewhere. Humans are migratory beings. Long before the westward movement, people migrated to richer pastures in order to increase their quality of life and, in some cases, to survive. I am a strong proponent of thriving, not surviving.

With big business encroaching on middle America, education at a record low, healthcare costs seeming endless, poverty and unemployment at high levels, it's harder to break into the workforce no matter what degree you earned with quality of life on the decline, many people have decided now is the time to look elsewhere.

Below are a few important questions commonly asked by parents considering migration:

Would I be helping or hindering my children's growth and opportunities? Would we be able to return if we decided it was best for the kids? Is it safe? What is the cost of school?

Moving your family from your place of residence is an extremely personal decision. My goal is to fully inform and answer any questions you have so you can make the best decision for your family. Remember, no decision is a decision in itself. Now, let's address these common concerns.

«EDUCATION ABROAD»

The most important criteria for many expat parents is accreditation. They want their children to have as many options and open doors as possible.

There are a few degree options your children can earn while attending school in Mexico:

The International Baccalaureate (IB) Diploma, accredited by the International Baccalaureate Organization in Geneva Switzerland, is the most flexible option. This degree makes your kids eligible to apply for college in the USA, Europe, and Latin America.

The local high school diploma which makes your child eligible to apply for college in-country. In order to attend college in the US, they would need to take the GED exam.

The USA High School Diploma is available at most American private schools and online through the various homeschool programs (i.e. K-12). This diploma enables you to apply to colleges in the USA, Europe, and many other countries. It's essentially the same degree your child would have earned had they stayed in the US.

Expats have the same three options for schooling that their peers have in their hometown: homeschool, private school, and public school. You should know that Mexico doesn't refer to the various school steps as you're accustomed. Instead they use the terms: basic education (preschool- 9th grade), upper secondary education (3 year high school or professional technical program), and tertiary education (Bachelor degrees, specialized training, teacher certificate, master degrees, and doctorates).

Foreigners often decide to place their children in private English taught schools so their child acclimates more smoothly, without a language barrier. Others opt for full immersion through placement in Spanish speaking schools so their children will become bi-lingual more quickly. The latter option is harder for the first six months to a year but after the hump, your kids are bi-lingual and thereby can acclimate easier with their new friends using their newly acquired language skills.

There are a variety of ways to homeschool and obtain a US or IB diploma for little to no money! Also, there are numerous private English-taught schools in Mexico.

HOMESCHOOLING

Homeschooling has gained popularity both in the States and abroad. The only difference is really where "home" is. Homeschooling abroad can be challenging when considering activities designed for groups of participants of the same age.

K-12.com

This site allows you to navigate through international education options from a variety of schools ranging from public to preparatory. If you maintain an address in the US and pay taxes in that state *(maybe a family member's address for your mail)*, you can select the corresponding state and enroll in online public school.

Many states require you to start the program while in-state, so make sure to set up your education options before you leave the area. In-person "Start-Up Success" sessions are often provided to introduce the student to the online learning setting while you're there.

They also develop customized Individualized Learning Plans (ILP). If your program requires textbooks, make sure and get as many as you can prior to leaving. Purchasing books and shipping them to Mexico can be a bit of a hassle (see *Mail* in the *Before You Leave* section).

Most K-12 programs offer college level courses so your child can earn college credits while in high school!

Go to www.k-12.com to learn more.

PUBLIC SCHOOLS

Would I be helping or hindering my children's growth and opportunities?

Don't take my word for it. Schedule an appointment with potential colleges and employers in respectable fields. Ask them how they would respond to a potential student or employee with international experience.

What I believe you will discover is that an international upbringing adds quality, diversity, and growth that no other program or school could match.

At the very least, your child will be bi-lingual in what many consider as the top two most powerful languages. Spanish is the official language of 21 countries. He or she would have successfully acclimated into another culture and way of life (huge points in both college entry and employment), and they would have learned life skills and experienced self-growth unmatched by a peer that remained in their home country. I would have loved an international upbringing.

Outside of resumés and college entry brownie points, your child will learn about nature by experiencing it with all five senses! There's no museum required in order to experience biology in Mexico. Gone are the days when the football team receives the majority of the school's budget.

Home life could refocus around the family. An affordable family-centric life is the norm and the expected way of life in Mexico. Since life is less expensive, you're free to take breaks from your work to play with, talk to, and shape your own children's lives! Gone are the days of depending on daycare or school to raise YOUR children, a dream come true for many!

Your path will not be without bumps. The transition time may be very difficult on you and your kids. If your kids are adolescents, it can be particularly rough. Language acquisition will be harder and their self-consciousness will hinder their language expression. Teenagers undoubtedly experience hardship finding their place in the world. They want to be different and the same all at once. If you add a new culture and language into an already volatile time, you can expect an explosion.

That being said, every child is unique and how they handle change can be dramatically different from child to child. I've spoken to many parents who've said their kids are happier than they've ever been. I've also seen some who have expressed that their child feels a little out of place.

EXPAT EXPERIENCE

Listen to our podcast, Episode 9 where Katie O'Grady (mom, wife, blogger, and retired Spanish teacher) shares why she felt it necessary to homeschool her kids in San Diego and yet in Mexico found the public education system to be just what she was looking for to raise her twins.

www.movingabroadpodcast.com

www.losogradysinmexico.com

Moving abroad could be the best thing you could do for your teenager. Only you know what's best for your kids. Don't let society or me tell you what your kids need.

Would we be able to return if we decided that it was best for the kids?

The answer to this question is very much dependent on your planning. If you're not fully committed to the idea of moving your family abroad, why not commit to a year? Save up enough emergency cash to fly everyone home and pay for at least three months of bills.

If you own your home and have gained a handsome amount of equity, you have a choice to make. You can either cash out, have your safety pile of cash, and rent in Mexico, or you can hire a rental agency to rent your US home and rent in Mexico.

The risk is not equal for each option. If you choose the cash out option and Mexico doesn't work out, then you could possibly have a difficult time finding a comparable house or the same interest rate you locked into years ago.

The market, however, is unpredictable. Take the market in 2002, for example. If you had sold and moved away from California just before the crash, you would have likely doubled your money! Decide what's most important to you, the money upfront or the security of owning a home with potential rental income.

As far as schooling goes, if you were homeschooling, your kids won't miss a beat. If your kids were in a Mexican school, there may be a bit of re-acclimation but no unsurpassable hurdles there.

Work

As far as work is concerned, why not take your work with you? You would be surprised how many jobs are telecommuting friendly.[24] If your employer or your industry is not, start looking for something else that is, or start something new!

If you packed your work and took it with you then you would not be at risk of losing your income by moving abroad or globetrotting for that matter. In fact, the move would have increased your marketability. You could add: bi-lingual, an international specialist, or an international consultant on your brag list.

Is it safe?

Safety is on every parent's mind. I don't mean

---

[24] See the Telecommuting section for more information

to be too philosophical but what is safety? Do rules make it safe? Do low criminal statistics make it safe? Safety to me is a feeling, a vibe. I have felt very safe in countries with lax rules and dependency on the police. As mentioned in Basics, one expat said she felt safer in Mexico than in Ohio!

Your peers have likely bought in to the horrible media attention Mexico draws, which is arguably driven by political agenda. They might think you're crazy to even consider a move to Mexico, and that Mexico means certain death. Remind them that the US is the land of mass school murders, terrorist attacks, gangs, and other violent crimes.

In Mexico, children are free to roam the streets and play with the neighborhood kids without fear. While the cities are not crime free, the international norm is not fear-driven as it is in the US. To live life more freely, what a gift that could be to your child!

«ACCLIMATING THE CHILDREN»

Adjusting to a new school, language, activities, and exploration

If at all possible, plan your move so the kids have time to acclimate before school starts. Hire a private language tutor for them and you while you're still living in your home country. Make language acquisition a family endeavor. Play language Jeopardy, Apples to Apples (in the new language), or other language games together for game night

After arriving to your new country, sign up for intensive language classes as a family for at least two weeks, preferably a month.

You might not all be in the same class because your language levels may vary, but you will all be able to practice your Spanish together which will greatly assist your adjustment. If you or your spouse is struggling with the move, it will certainly reflect on your children's experience. So set yourself up for success.

ACTIVITIES

Make sure that moving abroad is an adventure for

the kids. You may have visited your country in the past and the kids enjoyed it as a vacation. This expectation is hard to come back from when transiting vacation life to real life. Make sure and plan fun activities.

Let them be part of the planning process. Give them assignments like "Explore the backyard and see if there would be a good spot for compost or a small garden." If they're old enough, have them research how to compost and build a compost bin / drum /stack for use in your yard. Find ways to connect their hobbies with the natural assets Mexico has to offer. My teenage brother-in-law built a zip-line and platform 50 feet up a tree with his dad! Other activities could include:

» Creating a scavenger hunt consisting of flora and fauna, birds, and frogs known to be in the area for them to take a picture of and identify. Then compare notes and see how many points they got! Reward the points with a trip to the beach, park, pool, or nearby waterfall!

» Bring a picnic to a nearby waterfall and enjoy the serenity.

» Feed the iguanas.

» Go on "adventure walks" together with a wildlife guidebook, learning and identifying new plants, insects, and animals each day.

» Take Spanish lessons from the same school and have homework sessions together.

» Once a month, let a child pick somewhere new to explore within a given range. If you can afford a weekend away once a month or once every two months, this would be a great way to get to know the country.

» Google "solar carving" and learn this fantastic way to use the sun's energy as your paint brush by engraving the wood through burning! A much better use of the magnifying glass than killing ants! Pick up a cheap pair of welding glasses from a hardware store.

» Buy cheap digital cameras (possibly disposable) and have photo contests! The winner gets to choose what's for dinner from a list of possibilities!

» Put a blanket down on the ground outside after dark and star gaze. Use an iPhone app, Skywalker, to help you identify the constellations. You can either tell the corresponding Greek mythology stories or make up new ones. You start the story then tag the person to your right to continue the story, and so on.

Key points to keep in mind are: language acquisition, change of schedule and expectations, making new friends, and getting them connected in the community so they have a sense of purpose. For teenagers, it is of utmost importance that they make it on their own. Support any healthy hobbies or interests they express. Make sure they have the freedom to find things that interest them.

When you run out of ideas, Pinterest is an excellent resource. Just search for things to do outside, craft ideas, gardening, things to do for free, and so on!

«WORK & BUSINESS»

A guide to starting a business abroad or operating one internationally

WORK HARD PLAY HARD

Not Retired?

You're never too young or too old to move to Mexico. It's a land for the wise, the adventurers, and the peace seekers. Herds of 20 and 30 somethings dissatisfied with the rat race are looking for alternative lifestyles elsewhere. There are also folks reinventing themselves in their retirement years by starting the business they always wanted.

Without the hurdles of large industry that encompass entrepreneurship in the US, an international startup is exceedingly more possible these days. Start up fees are modest, and because your new life in Mexico is significantly cheaper, you have more wiggle room in the first formative years of your business.

Whether your new business is registered in the US, Mexico, Hong Kong, or South Africa, you must satisfy a need in order for it to be successful.

Examine your market and see where gaps exist. If you hope to serve the community you live in, find out what needs are not being met. If you hope to serve an international community online, find a niche that you are passionate about and can easily satisfy from any location in the world.

Once you decide what type of business you want to create, set out with a business and marketing plan.

One side of my business entails filming and producing two minute marketing videos for adventure tours, destinations, hotels, real estate, and special events. In

Mexico, I can stroll into a hotel or tour agency with my iPad and easily obtain an audience with the decision maker and share what I can do for them.

In the US, it takes months of redirection, red tape, and dismissals before I may or may not gain an audience with the decision maker.

There's a huge market for tourism, niche group travel, retirement, medical tourism, eco-living, alternative living, health, and self-sustaining properties just to name a few.

Check out how your country performs in the World Bank Doing Business report for 2014,[25]

CREATING A BUSINESS ABROAD 101

Take time to consider the best way to incorporate and the location in which to file your business when you enter the world of entrepreneurship. Ask your experienced accountant about incorporating prior to doing so.

Incorporation requires a great deal of paperwork and expense and provides little to no benefits. Once incorporated, you are held accountable to countless ever changing laws and in order to dissolve the corporation, you will spend months completing the paperwork and nursing the resulting paper cuts. The take home message is really do your homework prior to taking action. Oftentimes it might be better to start out as a sole proprietor.

---

[25] For the full report:
http://www.doingbusiness.org/data/explore economies/ecuador

Consider your market. Are they locals, businesses, Canadians, or is your service or product without borders?

If after seeking counsel from experienced business owners and speaking with a local attorney, you have decided to start a business and register it in Mexico, you'll have a variety of things to do in order to make the ball roll. Some to-dos may include:

» Reserve the company name

» Hire a lawyer to prepare the minutes of incorporation

» Deposit capital into a bank account set up under the name of the company

» Have your lawyer present the documents above (with copies of the Charter and the Bylaws) to the appropriate party for the approval of the company's incorporation

» Publish an abstract of the charter in a daily newspaper that circulates where the company operates

» Apply for a tax ID

» Receive inspection and operations permit from the municipality

DOING BUSINESS

In order to be successful, you need to learn about your new home's work culture and how to incorporate it into the way you do business.

US and Canadian citizens are often quick firing, wheel and deal type of business people. If you're quick and to the point in the US, the time saved is greatly appreciated since time is the highest valued commodity. That business culture doesn't translate or get the job done in every country. Instead, regular social gatherings, sharing meals, and talking about your family might be what gets the job done.

Mexicans focus on trust. They can't trust what they don't know. Because of this, you may be drilled over every aspect of your private and public life before a local commits to working a deal with you.

Time management might also be drastically different in your new country than your hometown. In Mexico, your employees could arrive to meetings one to two hours late without apology (because it's the norm). The expectations are different in larger cities versus small pueblos. Learning to account for this rule will save you many headaches.

HIRING / FIRING EMPLOYEES ABROAD

Before you decide to hire locals for your business or to clean your house, study the labor laws carefully. They might be drastically different from the laws in your home country.

Make sure and create a well worded contract if you decide to employ a worker full-time.

The laws in Mexico favor the worker, so it's much more difficult to fire someone than hire someone. It's like a game of *Mother May I* but with much more paperwork. You can see why it's important to understand what you're getting into with a clear grasp of labor laws prior to hiring.

Many folks decide that for their small business it makes more sense to avoid all of the complications of hiring full-time staff by hiring independent contractors (IC). So instead of hiring two full-time workers, they might hire 4 ICs.

I hire ICs off of Elance, Odesk, and my new favorite, Fiverr.com to complete various skills for me: eBook formatting, cover art, design, logos, podcast edits and production, etc.

TELECOMMUTING

An increasing number of companies are seeing the win-win in telecommuting. They can lower overhead with utilities and real estate costs, and increase employee morale and productivity by allowing them to choose the environment where they thrive.

If your employer doesn't currently use telecommuters, don't worry, it doesn't mean they won't allow it. You must be savvy and take care how you present the offer. I recommend you read The Work From Home Handbook[26] by Diana Fitzpatrick and Stephen Fishman before you pitch to your boss. The book will help polish your pitch in order to speak their language and address their fears or concerns, before they even realized they had any.

If you don't have a job or your employer has closed the telecommuting door, then it may be time to look in another direction.

What are you experienced in? What can you bring to the table? Who would benefit from your skills? If you have worked in sales, how can you reshape

---

[26] http://bit.ly/workfromhomedf

yourself as an international asset?

INDEPENDENT CONSULTANT

If you have worked during your lifetime then you have experience in something. Think about what you're good at and see if you can pull together a market you can help through consultations.

There are a variety of business opportunities abroad with new business owners in every sector. These new owners need help with a variety of niches: marketing, social media, customer service practices, IT, website development, content creators, multi-media, international accounting, productivity, import/export, etc.

PROPERTY MANAGEMENT & REAL ESTATE

With more and more expats looking abroad to spend their "golden years" in a place that allows for a higher quality of life and young professionals looking for an international experience, real estate has opened up dramatically across the globe over the last few years.

With the wealthiest and largest group of people entering their retirement years, this market is expected to explode.

Don't expect to be signed as an exclusive buyer or seller agent. Look into the real estate culture and learn what are the norms.

In addition to sales, property management is also a promising market. That's not to say it's easy money. Anyone who has experience maintaining property in a foreign country will tell you that it's incredibly challenging and time consuming, especially if you don't have excellent handymen and a grasp of Spanish in your arsenal.

Numerous Mexicans and expats alike have second homes in Mexico. These homes need to be watched, maintained, and rented out in order to produce supplement an income. With the humidity along the coastal regions of Mexico, a house left unkept can literally rot.

TEACHING ENGLISH

You can easily earn your TESOL or TEFL certificate online or in the classroom, making you eligible to apply for teaching jobs around the world. Most employers require you to be a native English speaker, and have taken a 120 hour course in either TESOL or TEFL. Some also require a Bachelor's degree in any subject.

While taking your TEFL certification, it's possible to specialize in "young learner" or "business English" thereby adding marketability and greater appeal to land a job in your preferred target audience.

I received my TESOL certificate through International TEFL and TESOL Training. I chose the 120 unit course and completed it online with my spouse. They allowed us to turn in one homework per unit since we would be completing it together. Each assignment we turned in was reviewed by our tutor, Earl. If any changes needed to be made, Earl sent it back with remarks. I have no complaints and would recommend them:

http://bit.ly/TEFLTESOL

NGOs & FOUNDATIONS

The international NGO (non-government

organization) community is enormous. Many of these organizations are in need of English speaking staff in administration, fundraising, marketing, and other job classifications. Monthly salary can range greatly.

TOURISM JOBS

Tourism is a multi-billion dollar industry. As mentioned before, the baby boomers are just beginning to enter into their retirement as the wealthiest group the world has ever seen. What do they all have in common? They all want to travel.

Group travel has always sported a healthy market and is seeing large increases in demand. This means you could hop on an established tour group as a tour director after you earn your certificate through the International Guide Academy: www.bepaidtotravel.com).

Or if you'd rather guide than direct, become a specialized guide for a niche group: LGBT, Food, Wine, Coffee, Grandparent, or Children tours to name a few. You can earn guide certification through the National Tour Association: www.ntaonline.com. In addition to an international license, you might need to obtain your certification as a tour guide from the Ministry of Tourism in your country.

If you're a *behind the scenes* kind of person and have an artistic eye, you can secure work designing those flashy tourism brochures and website content.

WORK VISAS

Securing a work visa usually requires you to demonstrate that you are filling a position a local does not have the capabilities to fill (i.e. English language, healthcare, IT, Biotech, and

International Business skills).

You will need a letter from the company is offering you a position specifying why they are contracting you and what importance you will bring to their company.

JOBS "OFF THE BOOKS"

Under the table jobs are more often sought out by younger folks without kids. This book does not endorse working illegally, it simply acknowledges that it occurs. Undocumented jobs often include: restaurant work, bi-lingual tourism jobs (often owned by expats), flier distributer, sales, marketing, etc.

VIRTUAL OFFICE 101

Telecommuting, independent contracting, creative arts, and the freedoms provided by the worldwide web, make working from any location around the world limited only by your creativity and bandwidth.[27]

In order to work from your dream location, you will need to establish a framework. This can include but is not limited to setting up an email account, online banking, international communication solutions, business numbers in each country code necessary, mail forwarding services, securing a US address, purchasing a laptop and any devices required for connectivity to the internet.[28]

After the basics are set up, you will need to create an environment conducive

---

[27] Internet signal strength

[28] Cable modem, wireless router, booster, or hot spot device

to work and productivity. A space free from distractions, one that you can also walk away from when it's quitting time. Consider what you want your work hours to be? Are you more creative and productive in the morning or late at night?

Many 8 to 5'ers are not accustomed to the variety and freedoms allotted to those who work from home. Find out what works best for you. Experiment with your schedule until you find the best flow.

Most people feel their best with a regular sleep and rise schedule, a morning shower, eat breakfast, and get dressed for the day before they attempt to contribute to society. This is still true if you work from home. Just because you can work in your PJs doesn't necessarily mean you should.

Do not neglect your self-care each day. Take time to exercise, eat, and take breaks. It's absolutely imperative that you have a start and stop time! Telecommuting doesn't mandate that you work 24 hours a day. Just because your office and laptop are one room away, doesn't mean you are on call 24/7. You need to set clear boundaries for yourself and those you work with. Creating a balanced schedule and sticking to it is key for a successful balance of life, family, and business.

A friend of mine, Corey Coates, owns a Podcast production company (Podfly) in addition to working for a second company as a program director. He shared,

"I start every workday early with yoga, meditation, and a light breakfast (fruit and yogurt). Then I work until lunch, when I leave for a stroll on the beach. I then return to work until 3:30pm, quitting time. I turn my phone off, close my laptop and don't think of work a minute after 3:30pm. That's the key to being as productive as I am, and not burned out."

ONLINE BANKING

Make sure your bank allows you to bill-pay, fax wire transfer information, and charges zero or minimal currency transactions fees. At the time of writing, Charles Schwab offered a High Yield Investor Checking account with no monthly service fees or minimums, no foreign transaction fees, unlimited ATM fee rebates worldwide, mobile deposits from your smartphone, and FDIC insurance up to $250,000! See **Banking** in the **Before you Leave** section for more information.

COMMUNICATION

Business would not exist without communication. Your business may require both local and international communication options.

Let's begin with phone communication. How's your internet connection? If your service is reliable and your electricity rarely fails, then Skype and magicJack could be excellent options for an international phone solution. If you maintain international clients, you can purchase a phone number with the desired country and area code for a one time annual fee through Skype. You could then forward all of those numbers to funnel through the same phone with the use of Google Voice. If you plan to serve the local community then you need to have an local number, most likely a cell phone for smaller one person operations.

I purchased a San Diego area code number from Skype for $60 USD for a year subscription. In addition to a US number, I was given 3 way calling, group video conferencing, and a personal voicemail. As with any internet phone service, there are glitches from time to time. I've had a few instances where my voicemail didn't pick up, and my client was unable to leave a message, but it is a rare occurrence.

With Skype, the customer can buy a subscription for just about any type of unlimited calling they desire: North America, Latin America, and world wide all starting at $2.99 per month!

If you have a smartphone and a local sim card installed,[29] download the Skype app. Once you are logged in and have a strong connection to the internet through either cellular or wifi, you are able to use all of your Skype features on the go!

VIRTUAL ADMIN SUPPORT

There are a variety of administrative support options available virtually. Packages range from answering services to full-time virtual assistants (VAs). Answering services start at just 80¢ a day including a friendly operator answering the phone with your company's name. Afterwards, they either forward the call or take a message then email and/or fax the message to you. ReceptionHQ has an iPhone app that allows you to change receptionist settings and diversion numbers from anywhere in the world. They offer a free seven day trial. Try them out before you leave the country and see what you think.

http://www.receptionhq.com

A virtual assistant (VA) is exactly what it sounds like, a private secretary that works from his/her home. They can answer and respond to phone calls, filter through and answer your emails, and redirect the ones that require your special attention. Common tasks also include: booking

---

[29] See *Logistics* for more information about local sim cards

your travel, managing your personal and professional calendar, managing social media, blogging, chat room presence, and running down leads.

Tim Ferriss emphasized the usefulness of VAs in his book The 4-Hour Work Week.[30] One example of a VA company is EAHelp http://bit.ly/USVAs. They provide an executive assistant starting with as little as five hours a week. I have had great luck hiring people from Elance.com and odesk.com for administrative and creative tasks.

---

[30] http://bit.ly/4hrworkweekbook

«TAXES, CORPS, & BANKING»

Tricks for currency conversion, insights on taxes and reporting, & an introduction to Mexican banking

"PAYING THE MAN"

If you register your company with Mexico, make sure and learn the tax filing requirements and penalties of your type of organization. Hire a local CPA that has raving reviews from other business owners.

In addition to annual corporate taxes, many companies are required to report monthly! Even if you didn't make a dime, you must report what you did or did not make each month. Some countries will even fine you if you are just one day late!

INTERNATIONAL TAX

There are a variety of proposals being thrown around worldwide to create an international tax or tax on a company/individual's worldwide income. The provocation for change is international multi-million dollar companies including Google, Starbucks, and rich individuals who have given up their US citizenship just before receiving a large sum of money from an investment or inheritance while utilizing international shields to dodge paying taxes.

The United States and other developed countries are trying to reel in control of these mega offshore companies and expat businesses get caught in the crossfire at times.

In 2013, the US saw more than double the number of people emigrating than any other full year in the history of the United States, over 3,000 people. This shift is believed to be due to a 2010 law entitled the Foreign Account Tax Compliance Act (FATCA) which was implemented in 2014. FATCA makes it 'legal' for the US to bully financial institutions around the world into providing account numbers of clients who hold US citizenship. This information is then sent to the good ole' IRS. Read more about FATCA in the *US Tax* section.

As of this writing, there are no taxes on worldwide income. By definition, an international tax would create double taxation. If the US is successful in creating it, they will be able to add double taxation to Washington D.C.'s taxation without representation faux pa. Keep your eye on this issue if you own an international business or have assets in a foreign bank.

David McKeegan is the cofounder of Greenback Tax Services,[31] an international company specializing in tax preparation for US citizens living elsewhere. I have

[31] check them out:
www.greenbacktaxservices.com

vetted him and had a blast doing it. I really place my stamp of approval on him and his services. Check out our recent podcast interview at www.movingabroadpodcast.com. (I'm not an affiliate or get renumeration in any way besides enjoying the company of a fun and helpful person).

times are changing. The assumption is if you are moving large sums of money out of North America, especially the US, then you must be doing something naughty with it. Since FACTA[32] passed, banks are required to ask you what you're doing with *your* money as if that's any of their business!

MOVING MONEY

♦ Western Union

An oldie but goodie at times. Western Union cuts out the middle man and allows you to send money to people around the world.

♦ Wire Transfer

This is the most used and simplest way to send larger sums of money into the country. Unfortunately,

♦ **Paypal**

Paypal can be a great way to get paid for a service or product, however, you must link it to a US bank account. So, if you're looking for a US-free financial solution, this isn't it. It also doesn't allow you to run international credit cards.

♦ **Wells Fargo**

Wells Fargo has an option called "Express Send." You can wire money

---

32
http://www.irs.gov/Businesses/Corporation
s/Foreign-Account-Tax-Compliance-Act-FATCA

online from your US account to participating banks around the world for just $9. Not only is it a great rate but it's called express for a reason, it arrives in less than an hour! In order to set up *Express Send,* you must go through a two week set up process but it's worth it! They also have an account package called the PMA package[33] that allows you two fee-free ATM withdrawals per statement period. The PMA package has a $30 monthly fee that is waived if you maintain at least $25,000 in your account.

If you send money to a bank that's not on their "special list" then they charge the industry standard $40-$50.

US TAXES

It doesn't take a tax professional to recognize that the US wants their cut of the pie. Even though you have left the States, they will still tax you. Some expats have given up their citizenship in an effort to avoid paying taxes to a country they do not live in. If your worth is greater than $622,000 and you gave up your citizenship, you may be pursued by the IRS for tax evasion. The US has even gone so far as to create an Expatriation Tax which requires the expat who has renounced their citizenship to pay taxes for 10 years after they are no longer a US citizen!

Since the US is losing people from the highest tax brackets to other countries, they have enacted a new law to deter others from emigrating. You are no longer allowed to reacquire your citizenship once you renounce it! Seems like the government holds a grudge!

---

[33] http://bit.ly/fargoPMA

FATCA- *Foreign Account Tax Compliance Act*[34]

FATCA is a government response to heavyweight tax evaders. A provision as recent as July 1, 2014 was initiated through FATCA *requiring* foreign financial institutions with US clients to provide annual reports to the IRS with the name, address, largest account balance of the year, and total debits and credits of any account owned by their US customer. The new law is a way for the United States to monitor where you are, how much money you have, and impose a 30% withholding tax for institutions concerning U.S. securities who do not comply.

It's going to be a roller coaster ride watching this dramatic new law play out. Only time will tell how big of a mess we will end up in. Hundreds of international banks have closed the accounts of their US customers due to the outrageous demands by the US (FATCA).

You can file your US tax return through a US Embassy or mail it.[35]

FOREIGN EARNED INCOME EXCLUSION
for US citizens

A potential break in the aggressive US tax requirements is the Foreign Earned Income Exclusion. In order to qualify, you must be a US citizen and either be a "bona fide resident" of a non-US country (hold a resident card and live full time in another country), or have spent ≥330 full days in a country other than the US during a period of 12 months. The days are in total, they do not have to be

---

[34] To read the argument why FATCA is bad for Amercia go to: http://bit.ly/FATCAbad

[35] Go to the IRS website, U.S. Citizens and Resident Aliens Abroad section for more information.

consecutive, and are not reset on January 1st. In any 12 month span, you must have been in another country to qualify. Travel days in international water or on a plane do not count towards your 330. This system is self-recorded but if you are audited, they will look at things like passport entrance/exits and so on.

If you qualify for FEIE, you won't have to pay taxes on income of $99,200 or less (for 2014, it will break the 6-digit mark in 2015). You may also qualify to deduct foreign housing costs. The annual cap for the housing exclusion is roughly $29,760 or 30% of the maximum Foreign Earned Income Exclusion. Remodeling, decorating, and furnishing is not included.

If you qualify for the exclusion, it doesn't mean you don't have to file taxes. You are required to file if you made more than $9,750 in worldwide income. You may not pay a dime, but

Uncle Sam wants to keep an eye on you.

The most popular tax forms for the expat are the standard 1040, Form 2555- Foreign Earned Income Exclusion and the Form 1116- Foreign Tax credit.

The rules for this exclusion are not simple. I would recommend using a CPA or other tax professional who specializes in expatriate taxes. This section is in no way to be used as the sole reference for tax guidance. It's simply a gringo's take on expat taxes as best I can understand. *See www.becominganexpat.com for CPAs and attorneys vouched for by expats.*

FBAR

Report of Foreign Bank & Financial Accounts[36]

Any US citizen that has over $10,000 in accumulative accounts

[36] http://bit.ly/FBARtax

outside of the US at anytime during the calendar year is required to report it to the US government. Even if it was for the purchase of a house, and you simply transferred the money into your international bank account where it was immediately routed out during escrow.

The filing deadline is June 30th every year. In 2014 the US changed the filing making it mandatory to file online. You will need to download free Adobe Acrobat if your computer doesn't already have it.

CANADIAN TAX CONSIDERATIONS37

If you're Canadian and planning a move to Mexico, the government wants you to inform the Canada Revenue Agency (CRA) before you leave to work out what your residency status will be. They have a form to help you decide what status fits your situation: NR73. Numerous Canadian expats follow the stance that they can decide what their residency status is for themselves and opt not to share information.

In order to keep your GSI (Guaranteed Income Supplement) you cannot be outside of Canada for more than six months out of the year. Below is a list of other deal breakers that would result in the loss of your GSI:

» You don't file an individual Income Tax and Benefit Return by April 30, or if, by the end of June each year, they have not received the information about your net income for the previous year

» You leave Canada for more than six consecutive months

---

37 http://bit.ly/CanuckImmigration

» Your net income is above the <u>maximum annual</u>[38] income

» You are incarcerated in a federal penitentiary for two years or longer

» You die (morbid but true)

I always advise to consult your tax professional with important decisions such as this one. Reading through governmental jargon is seemingly impossible to decipher. So if the below bullet-points leave you scratching your head or throwing this book across the room, just leave it to the professionals.

The information below covers each resident status in Canada and is quoted from a Canadian governmental website: <u>travel.gc.ca</u>

♦ **Factual residents**

» Working temporarily outside Canada

» Teaching or attending school in another country

» Commuting (going back and forth daily or weekly) from Canada to your place of work in the United States, or

» Vacationing outside Canada

♦ **Deemed residents**

» A federal, provincial or territorial government employee who was a resident of Canada just before being posted abroad or who received a representation allowance for the year

» A member of the Canadian Forces

» A member of the Canadian Forces overseas school staff

---

[38] <u>http://bit.ly/maxlimit</u>

who chooses to file a return as a resident of Canada

» Working under a Canada International Development Agency assistance program if you were a resident of Canada at any time during the three-month period just before you began your duties abroad

» A dependent child of one of the four persons described above and your net income for the year was not more than the basic personal amount (line 300 in the General Income Tax and Benefit Guide) or

» A person who, under an agreement or convention (including a tax treaty) between Canada and another country, is exempt from tax in that other country on 90% or more of their income from all sources because of their relationship to a resident (including a deemed resident) of Canada

◆ **Non-residents**

» Normally or routinely live in another country and are not considered a resident of Canada

» Do not have significant residential ties to Canada, and

» Live outside Canada throughout the tax year, or

» Stay in Canada for less than 183 days in the tax year

◆ **Deemed non-residents**

» If you are a factual resident or a deemed resident of Canada and are considered to be a resident of another country that has a tax treaty with Canada, you may be considered a deemed non-resident of

Canada for income tax purposes.

BRITISH PENSIONS

QROPS & QNUPS[39] are two five letter acronyms every British expat should know.

QROPS stands for Qualifying Recognized Overseas Pension Scheme, but is often called an 'offshore' pension because the providers of said pension work from financial centers around the world.

There are more than 3,000 options available across 46 countries. Some expats opt to work with a financial adviser instead of dealing directly with a QROPS provider. There are various rules and tax implications depending on the laws of the country where the program is based.

Reasons why a Brit might want to consider a QROPS include:

» up to 30% lump sum availability

» inherent tax free

» portability

QNUPS stands for Qualifying Non-UK Pension Scheme. The two programs are very similar, consult your financial advisor to decide which is better for you and your family.

[39] http://bit.ly/UKexpatpension

«HOW TO LIVE FOR FREE»

Work trades and house-sitting

Living for free is not a myth or a gimmick. People are living rent and food free across the globe. This lifestyle is temporary for some and permanent for others! It can serve in financial hardship or offer an alternative lifestyle for folks who aren't attached to things, locations, and consumerism. It certainly pulls at the heartstrings of nomads.

Whatever the reason, whatever your situation, it's possible so unless you're attached to the idea of paying rent, it would be crazy not to consider!

HOUSE-HOTEL-PET-SITTING

Exactly as it sounds, if you are a house, hotel, or pet sitter, you watch and maintain the property and animals per the instructions of the owner. If you do your homework right, this type of arrangement is a win win and can be an excellent way to save money while experiencing life as a local in a new area!

There is a huge range of responsibilities from one sitting job to another. Which is why it's imperative to ask all of the right questions, gather all the information, rules, and expectations before you commit to a job. Your tasks could range from watching a house and watering plants, to a rigorous pet activity and care program that requires something of you every couple of hours. Below are some examples of websites that advertise care-taking jobs. While options in Mexico exists, none of the sites exist solely for Mexico and their inventory constantly turns over.

♦ **MindmyHouse.com**

$20/year

♦ **HouseCarers.com**

$50/year

This site has room for improvement, but is an excellent choice for those seeking a house in Australia

♦ **CareTaker.org**

$30/year

I have personally used this site, and find that it has extensive listings. The downside is it doesn't allow you to view all of the listings without subscribing.

♦ **TrustedHouseSitters.com**

$49 for 3 months

$64.00 for 6 months

$79.00 for12 months

This site offers more listings than any of the others.

Word of Mouth & Part-Time Expats

Keep your eyes and ears open for opportunities to help other expats keep their home and pets safe while they visit family back home!

You will have to put forth some effort to land a house/pet sitting gig. After all, living for free is a pretty epic goal and competition can be fierce. The first job is often the hardest to land because you lack experience and pertinent references. The key to success is to look at each sitting opportunity as a job interview. Be professional, polite, and learn as much about the position as possible before you make any decisions.

The profile you create (with the service you subscribe to) is the equivalent of your resume. If you don't put in effort here, don't bother subscribing. Remember, these home and pet owners are looking for a stranger to welcome into their home when they aren't going to be there! Don't sound like a robot, be yourself in a respectable way and show passion. Let them get to know you through your profile.

Include examples that display how responsible you are: your hobbies, your cleanliness, pet enthusiasm, experience, your hobbies, and what you can do for them. Don't just say you like dogs, make sure and use examples demonstrating how much you care for animals (i.e. you're a volunteer for a local humane society). If you have horse, gardening, or farming experience, say so. If you haven't worked as a house/ pet sitter abroad, but have done so for family and friends include those experiences and offer the references. If you have experience with www.couchsurfing.org, make sure to include that along with your user name then the homeowners can read your reviews as a guest and host on the site. When in doubt, ask previous bosses, landlords, and even teachers to vouch for your trustworthiness and reliability.

Everyone has a special set of skills, if your's happens to be handy work, then mention it. Homeowners will feel better knowing their home will be cared for if something breaks while they are away. If you have gardening skills, marketing skills, computer skills, alternative energy skills, list them. You never know how your skills could benefit the homeowner. After all, the goal here is a mutually beneficial relationship!

Once you find a job you want to apply for, you have a chance to send a brief message along with your profile for their review. Treat this message like a cover letter. A brief introduction to what you can do for them, why their house is the job you want, and why they should hire you over other prospective sitters. Make sure to be passionate and real. Show your personality in a professional way.

Speaking of professionalism, make sure to respond quickly and professionally to each email correspondence. Write their name at the top, use full sentences, and always end your message with something to the effect of, "I appreciate your time and consideration."

Hesitation may cost you excellent housesitting opportunities. If the house is in a desirable location, the position will often be filled the same day it posts. Setting up alerts for your desired location could be the most important thing you do with your service.

Once you have captured a homeowner's interest and have answered their questions or concerns, don't neglect your own. You need to ask the right questions to insure the position is a good fit for you. Ask the owner:

» Is it ok to have guests?

» How long can the pet/house be left alone? (You may wish to explore a nearby town for the weekend)

» Is there a vehicle you can use?

» What is public transit like near them?

» How far away is the nearest grocery store?

» Will you have access to the internet?

» Is there warm water?

» Are there any rules you need to abide by?

MASTERING SITTING

In order to be an excellent house/pet sitter, all that's required is common sense and fullfillment of the owner's requests. Remember, you're a guest so make sure you return the home in *better* condition than you received it. Wash the linens you used, make certain the house is tidy, and if you'd like some brownie points, make some brownies! Leave something homemade in the fridge for their arrival home with a note so they know you made it especially for them.

Pay close attention to the owner's requests. If the owner asks you to leave the mail in a certain area, take care to neatly place the mail in its designated place. If they'd like you to check in via email every so often, make sure and set an alarm in your calendar to do so. If you respect their wishes and go above and beyond the minimum expectation, you will accumulate an unending list of glowing references enabling a rent-free lifestyle for as long as you'd like.

WORK EXCHANGE

A work exchange is bartering work for accommodations. It's a great opportunity to see what it's like to live and work in a new region or with a new culture without taking financial risk.

Workaway.info and Helpx.net are two great websites that allow you to search for places to work in exchange for free room and board *(On the flip side, once you decide to buy a home, you can host workers through the site to help you remodel, or advertise a new business in exchange for room and board.)*

Just like housesitting, your profile matters! Take time to construct one that really draws on your skillset. Next, search the country where you'd like to work and the type of work that you'd like to do.

For example, I searched Mexico and organic farm stay. This resulted is a list of organic farm owners who were looking for some extra help in exchange for room and board. The range of work possibilities is extensive. Examples of work projects include: help with new construction, marketing, refurbishing a boat, gardening, cooking, teaching English, farming, housekeeping, concierge, working with horses, etc.

The most common arrangement I've seen advertised is approximately 20 hours of work in exchange for free room and board. I'd also say that farming both organic and in-organic offer the most jobs.

Make sure and clarify your specific arrangement with the owner because every situation is unique. Some work exchanges are full-time in exchange for free room and board and an additional stipend. I've seen others that want you to pay them for some of your expenses and work full time for them.

Free room and board is great, walking away from a few months living alongside a new culture, town, way of life, with a new skill, is priceless!

The Caretakers Gazette also offers work exchanges for a small stipend and free room and board. On that particular site, I've observed work as caregiver, handy-person, and live-in hotel manager most frequently.

COUCH SURFING

Couch surfing is not just a way to describe sleeping on your cousin's couch any longer. Now, it is an entire genre of travel. People of all ages travel around the world meeting Couch Surfers from every country they've traveled.

Couch surfing is a free short-term local housing solution. The average stay is two nights. It's a great way to travel around Mexico searching for the region that best suits you, and gathering information and advice from locals and expats who have already made the move.

www.CouchSurfing.org is a site whose slogan is, *"Changing the world one couch at a time."* To experience this new way of travel, all you need to do is sign up and create a free profile. There, you can decide whether you'd like to host travelers, play tour guide, or simply chat over a cup of joe, and exchange stories.

You're never required to host someone, even if your profile says that you can.

You can search for potential hosts, or for *surfers* looking for a place to stay in your area. If you find a "couch" you'd like to surf, simply write to them.

In your couch surfing request, tell them why you'd like to stay with them in particular. Show them that you took the time to read their profile.

Even though it's called "couch" surfing, oftentimes your host has a spare bedroom you can have all to yourself! The sleeping situation is listed in the profile of the potential host.

I've couch surfed in Canada, St. Lucia, and across the United States. I have hosted surfers many times in Costa Rica and had excellent experiences making friends with travel peers around the world!

ADDITIONAL READING

Work Your Way Around the World: The Globetrotter's Bible by *Susan Griffith*

Remote: Office Not Required by *Jason Fried & David Heinemeier Hansson*

«HEALTHCARE & GOLDEN YEARS»

An introduction to healthcare, supplemental insurance, retirement, & the part-time expat

HEALTHCARE

Healthcare is a big deal for most. Take a look at elections across the globe, a leading promise is always to better healthcare. Why? Because it matters. We want the assurance if we get sick and are in need of care or a life saving procedure, we will have access. In addition to a language and culture barrier, your new country will have a health system unfamiliar to you.

Healthcare is quirky and personal. Each individual's comfort level will vary. Some folks prefer to pay out of pocket and others choose to purchase a combination of public, private, and international healthcare insurances. Each plan carries a corresponding price tag and peace of mind.

Mexico's healthcare system is a hodgepodge of small private healthcare intermixed with universal and international health insurance programs. Private, public, and employer-funded healthcare schemes exist side by side. In addition, state employees and military personnel have an entirely unique insurance setup, similar to our congressmen and women in the US.

PREVENTION

Below are a few illness prevention techniques:

» Take daily walks through your new natural oasis and see your mood, energy level, bone density, Vitamin D levels, and health improve.

» Replace sugar drinks and beer with fresh coconut water (coco helado) and smoothies made from the ridiculously delicious produce. (If you're in the tropics)

VACCINATIONS

It's a good idea to go to a travel clinic or schedule an appointment with your doctor in order to discuss and receive vaccinations. Look at the **CDC** site for more information. Their recommended vaccinations include:

» Hepatitis A

» Typhoid

» Hepatitis B

» Rabies *(for those who plan to work with dogs, live in remote areas, adventure travel, or caving)*

» Malaria

If you have any questions or other concerns about vaccinations and other health precautions (i.e. safe food, water practices,

and insect bite protection) call the Centers for Disease Control and Prevention's hotline: 1-877-FYI-TRIP (1-877-394-8747).

CARE

Sometimes, the right healthcare option for you is a matter of comfort. If you've had the same cardiologist or family practitioner for years, you have a history and trust that was built over the course of many years. Moving abroad will reset that comfort level. In order to manage this change, I highly recommend you interview doctors during your *"try before you pry"* time. Make an appointment and interview specialists that are applicable to your needs.

INTERVIEW YOUR DOCTOR:

» Where did they complete schooling?

» Are they board certified? *(All physicians are licensed but not all are board certified.)* If so, in what specialty?

» How many patients have they had with my particular ailment/ condition?

» How can you reach them outside of office hours? Cell phone number?

» Do they respond to calls during office hours?

» If they are out of town, who fills in for them?

» What is their philosophy of healthcare?

» Do they have more than one location to see patients?

» How do they handle billing?

After you have collected all of your information with at least three physicians (preferably those you have been referred to), decide what questions and answers hold the most stout with you and score them accordingly. Don't forget to weigh in heavily with your comfort level and rapport with your future physician.

PUBLIC HEALTHCARE

In 2004 Mexico began to bolster it's public healthcare system through a program called *Seguro Popular*. The goal behind the program was to provide low cost access to healthcare for the poor. Statistics show that it's working. Since its inception, there have been over 50 million people treated who previously went without medical care.

If you decide to work and are hired by a Mexican company, you will likely pay into the Institute of Social Security. The amount will be based on your wages much like it is for social security and medicare tax in the US.

The Institute of Social Security is not only a lockbox of money, it operates its own primary care units and hospitals. Make sure and tour their facilities near the locations you're considering a move to because the quality varies drastically. Because it's a public Mexican service, the staff is often monolingual Spanish speakers. You'll find many more English speaking options in the private sector.

IMSS (inexpensive national healthcare)

♦ **2014 fees PER YEAR:**

0-19 years:	$111
20-29 years:	$132
30-39 years:	$139
40-49 years:	$198
50-59 years:	$212
60-69 years:	$306
70-79 years:	$320
80 + years:	$323

(fees increase in Feb of each year)

This program is sufficient for many. You will have drastic savings on prescription medicines (**free** when prescribed by an IMSS doctor), minor procedures and regular check ups. As is the case for many public healthcare options, overcrowding may occur. Each region has a different demand, do some investigating about wait times and quality of offices in your area of consideration. Overcrowding is not the rule, there are times when you'll be able to just walk right in.

PRIVATE INSURANCE

OUT OF POCKET

Private healthcare abound in Mexico. One of the bigger hurdles is that all of the documents and contracts are often in Spanish so either you select with a great deal of trust or you take the contracts to your attorney to review. Private insurance grants access to high-quality services and special treatments.

Currently, the private health sector is still on the upswing. Especially in Mexico City, Guadalajara, and Monterrey, new hospitals are being built to provide specialized care and treatment to patients.

Monterrey, in relatively close proximity to the US border, has become the center of medical tourism. Here, US citizens try to escape the higher medical costs and more expensive treatments in their home country.

Healthcare abroad is often so cheap that healthy folks just opt to pay out of pocket. This is a common path for younger expats and those that don't mind gambling a bit. With office visits averaging $28, you can see why.

If you're concerned about cost, feel free to call the hospital where you would go and ask them the costs of a variety of procedures. They should have a fee schedule and will tell you the cost and the minimum you need to bring to get through the doors. Remember, in many countries, you won't be seen until you can prove payment. That fact can send those on the fence towards a government healthcare program where they know they're covered with a simple entrance of your residence card into the computer system, or private insurance where a simple confirmation phone call should do the trick.

INTERNATIONAL HEALTHCARE

There is a growing trend towards international lifestyles. If you don't plan to live in any one place full time or you travel so much you're rarely at home, an international plan might be a better option for you.

Make sure the plan you choose has coverage inside the US if you think you may need to return within the given time period. Many insurances omit the US due to its inflated healthcare expenses.

searching for airfare or car insurance. You enter in the ages of your family members and your desired international coverage. The most expensive factors seem to be whether or not you wish to have coverage in the US and whether or not you want to include emergency evacuation.

Before you settle on a program public, private, or otherwise, make sure you understand what is covered and what isn't. Some programs don't pay for "elective procedures" and consider a knee or hip replacement as prosthetic devices which are also not covered.

BROKERFISH

www.brokerfish.com

This is a search engine that you can use just like

INTERNATIONAL MEDICAL GROUP

IMG offers specialized packages for travelers and expats. Many plans offer coverage in Mexico and around the world, including the US and Canada. One of their customers shared their experience below:

"For us, the Working Gringos, who are in our early 50's, the cost is about $1400 USD a piece per year for coverage with any doctor in any hospital in the world. Of course, there is an option to pay monthly or quarterly as well. The requirement for most of these policies is that you must be living outside the United States when you get the insurance, and must be planning to live outside the United States for six months hence.

While we're sure that we were adequately insured when we bought our policy from GNP here in Merida, we paid almost $500 USD apiece for coverage similar to what we have now. But the entire package of documents was written in Spanish, making it very difficult for us to understand our policy and therefore, obtain any of our benefits.

If we had known about the policy available for expats that we have now, we certainly would have bought that from the beginning. If you are in the market for expat health insurance, we highly recommend IMG."

~ Ellen & James Field, expats from California

See the ad in the back of the book for who they purchased their plan through

TRAVEL INSURANCE

If you don't plan to "stay put" for longer than 6 months at any given time then travel insurance may be your best option. An added bonus to purchasing travel insurance besides coverage for your own flesh and bones, is you can opt for insurance against lost luggage, trip cancellation, and sometimes theft! This can be a great solution for those that only want emergency coverage. It also might be an ideal option for the part-time expat, see more in the *Part-Time Expat* section.

This is what suits my wife and I for the time being.

World Nomads offers amazing plans at affordable rates.

MEDICAL TOURISM

Three per cent of the *world*'s population travel internationally for medical treatment![40] That's roughly 211,710,000 people! Patients Beyond Borders, an organization that publishes international medical travel guidebooks, reported that

the medical tourism industry produces $40 billion a year in business.

Patients requiring elective, non-elective, and dental procedures are heading to Mexico. Procedures are often less than half the cost in the United States.

The medical tourism industry capitalizes where the US lacks. There are companies that will make all of your health and travel arrangements including taking you by hand to everywhere you need to be to accomplish your health needs.

BOOKS:

Patients Without Borders: Everybody's Guide to Affordable, World-Class Healthcare[41]

---

[40] IPK International Survey
[41] http://bit.ly/guidetohealthcare

«RETIRED LIFE»

Reinventing you, getting connected, falling back in love with life

Live in a place where as your age increases so does your level of respect from the community.

One size does not fit all, nor does one way of retiring fit every retired individual. This transition is not to be taken lightly. Just as your transition into adolescence, adulthood, and possibly parenthood were taken seriously so too should your transition into your wisest stage.

When considering a move to another country, you are in an ideal time to sit and reevaluate the person that you are today. Your life experiences have shaped you and groomed you to be who you are, don't base your decisions on the person you were in the 60s, 70s, or 80s. Instead, decide what is important to you now, and what do you want to be important to you now? Reshape your life based on your answers. Moving abroad gives you a unique gift, a reset button to recreate yourself. Don't waste it!

PRIORITIES

Homework time! Create a priority chart, listing no fewer than 15 priorities. Next to each priority, rate its importance with a 1 - 10 ranking, one representing the highest importance, ten representing the least. Some examples of priorities include: health, relationship, learning, location, spirituality, hobbies, financial security, travel, being active, giving back to the community, and family. Make a conscious effort to demonstrate your top ten priorities through time allocation.

After you have your core ten priorities, write down what success looks like in each one. For example, for health you could write: "Walk 3 miles every morning, attend yoga 2x weekly, and journal 4x weekly." This task will provide you with a way to measure your success.

Some of you may have lived for financial achievement and success, climbing the corporate ladder to the rooftop deck. You may feel a strong challenge to reshape what success looks like to you in this new stage of your life. You might not have support staff, meetings, and other daily procedures that create a sense of importance and success.

LEARN

You can't teach an old dog a new trick... Bullshit! Learn a new skill that you've always wanted to learn. Take up fly-fishing, birding, woodworking, basket weaving, hiking, or walking. Maybe you already have a few solid hobbies, take them to the next level. Buy that table saw or tool that you need to take your woodworking to the next level, or a sewing machine, new rod, or GPS device. Read a book on how to further expand your skills, watch YouTube tutorials or best yet, find an apprenticeship.

WHAT TO DO

You finally made it to retirement. Talk about the ultimate hurry up and wait. For most people, lounging by the pool all day sipping on piña coladas will be spectacular for about a week, then what? Hobbies only get you so far. What can you do that will give your life purpose? You could seek out volunteer opportunities within the community or a field of interest. Or you could pick up a part-time job.

It has become more and more common to see "retired" folks working part-time or stepping into the entrepreneur world by starting up a business they always dreamed about. Think about projects that would be fun. Look into part-time opportunities helping local businesses in your area through consulting or independent contractor work.

Get connected through social networks near you, both expat and local. Try not to isolate yourself into the expat world, you miss out on so much of what the local heart has to offer. Invite your neighbors over for dinner once a month, start up, or attend a "Sunday Funday" with your community.

Travel and explore your new country. There are rivers, waterfalls, forest, jungles to be seen! Don't watch them on the Discovery Channel, go out and find your passion.

When in doubt, give it time. For many it can take up to three years to fully adjust to a new culture. You have a lot of new adjustments: schedule, climate, latitude, culture, language, surroundings, activities, expectations, and so on.

If you find yourself growing disgruntled, take a "time out" and evaluate why. If you are resenting something that is and always was part of your country's individuality, try to change your perception and appreciate the country for what it is. Your new mantras could very well be: "I'm no longer in a rush", "Just roll with it," and "Look around, I'm in _____, who cares if the ___ takes forever!"

HEALTHY LIVING

Most countries don't need shows like the Biggest Loser because they have high quality affordable fruits, vegetables, rice, and beans served in place of burgers and fries.

Plus, it's hard not to be at least a little bit active in the tropics or country where you've opted out of your own vehicle. There are many gorgeous trails and empty beaches to explore by foot,

and if you're in the mountains, everywhere is uphill both ways!

The biggest challenge to maintaining a healthy lifestyle abroad is monitoring your alcohol intake.

LANGUAGE BARRIER

I mentioned in the regional section that there are a number of expat havens in Mexico where you can get by with little to no Spanish. However, making an effort to learn the language will open up countless possibilities and make your living experience immensely more enjoyable. Sign up for Spanish lessons whenever you can manage. Dedicate yourself to learning a word a day and integrating it in conversation. Watching movies in Spanish with English subtitles in order to train your ear. Listen to Spanish music. Whatever you do, don't get overwhelmed by the seemingly impossible task of learning another language. Do everything you can to slowly immerse yourself in the language and before you know it you'll be eavesdropping on scandalous café conversations.

I remember when I was learning Spanish living in Guatemala, I would finish the day absolutely exhausted. Trying to understand everything while facing a steep learning curve requires intense focus. Even when you become comfortable with the language, you can't simply tune out and still pick up everything that's going on in the background. The most important thing to keep in mind is not to be afraid to make mistakes! No one's going to laugh at you or turn up their nose, this isn't France.

If you move to a country that speaks a language other than your own, you are in for a bit of a challenge.

Tips for learning a new language:

For many adults, a major factor that slows down their language acquisition is fear of making mistakes. You didn't hear this from me but, a slight buzz can really lubricate the tongue and ease the perfectionism in you. It can also provide the liquid bravery needed to break through your learning plateaus. Too much alcohol and you can refer back to the previous section.

Picture a toddler learning English. They don't expect to get it right, so neither should the adult learner of a second language. They look adorable saying things wrong and you understand them. That will be you for awhile, an adorable gringo who is trying. More power to you!

LOVE LIFE

It's easy to fall into complacency, aiming at just surviving in life. Make a focused effort to rid your complacent habits and thrive, not survive! Experience each moment and appreciate what life is offering you in the now.

Fall into love with life again. Just as a relationship has to be watered time and time again to keep it fresh and alive, so too does your soul and outlook on life.

If you are single abroad, there is no reason why your perfect match isn't waiting for you in the next café. I am proof of this sentiment! I met my Utah born wife in Costa Rica! You really never know where you will meet that special someone.

It's never too late for love either! My favorite Canadians met in her 50s and his 60s, married, and couldn't be more in love! They no longer have to find a partner to sail, kayak, paddle, explore the world, and love life with!

EXPEL THE MONSTERS

Most Common Fears in Your Golden Years:

» You will outlive your money

» You will lose your marbles

» You will spend your last years alone

Take action with something you are passionate about as a direct rebuttal to fear. Taking action is the opposite of being a victim.

YOUR BETTER HALF

"I won't let him retire because then he'd drive me crazy!" I can't tell you how many times I have heard this from wives and husbands quoting why they can't retire (especially when I worked at a fire station). There are other options.

» Share at least one daily enthusiasm *(bird watching, cooking, volunteering, walking, swimming, kayaking, tennis, etc)*

» Keep yourselves in good shape

» Take responsibility for your own happiness

» Let go of old arguments

Recommended Books:

65 things to Do When You Retire [42]

The Retiring Mind,[43] Robert Delamontagne

The Couples Retirement Puzzle: 10 Must-Have Conversations for Transitioning to the Second half of Life[44] Robert Taylor and Dorian Mintzer

Aging Bravely, Shut Up and Stop Your Whining[45] by Dana Racinskas

---

[42] http://bit.ly/65tdretire
[43] http://bit.ly/retiringmind
[44] http://bit.ly/coupleconversations
[45] http://bit.ly/agingbravely

«THE PART-TIME EXPAT»

You're not quite ready for the plunge but would like to dabble a foot in?

Special considerations for seasonal expats

Does selling your home, your car, all of your belongings, kissing your kids and grandkids goodbye, and shipping out forever sound too drastic for you? It may seem impossible for you to live far from your family.

There is a middle ground. If you're a parent or grandparent, there is a good chance you have lived much of your life based around other's needs and desires. Now that your kids have kids, it's easy to get swallowed up into full-time child care and more responsibilities than you had imagined for *YOUR* golden years.

The choice is yours. If you decide you are going to chase your dreams then clearly define them and see where your family fits. If living an international life full-time is too much awayness, then how about snow-birding or halftime? Where is your balance? How long is the flight to your ideal location from your loved ones? Are there direct flights from the city where your children and grandchildren reside?

$$ LIFESTYLE

Can you afford the lifestyle you desire where you currently live on your retirement budget? If the answer is no, then ask yourself if you lived in an area overseas half of the year with more luxuries for less money would that help you fill the gap in your lifestyle goals?

Do you strive for continuity? For your six months abroad, will you want to return to the same country each time or do you think you will want the freedom to explore other affordable countries in the years to come? (if this is you, read Becoming a Nomad)

THE BALANCING ACT

Living in more than one location is inherently more work. There are double the utilities to turn on, off, and manage. If you rent out one or both of your homes, then you add an additional depth of complexity. Decorating, stocking, and maintaining homes in two countries can prove exhausting. In the end, most things worth doing are difficult. Living outside the box, in two boxes rather, may be the best arrangement for you and yours. Organization and planning are key components to help tame the additional responsibilities.

Good friends of mine, Lisa and Junior, have the goal of living a third of the year across three properties: their lake house in Virginia, their beach front estate in Roatan, and are currently looking for their third spot (potentially in Ecuador). They plan to rent each property while they are away, creating a passive income while living their dream. They have it figured out!

PROPERTY MANAGEMENT

For those who opt to purchase homes, rental income can be an excellent option. Vacation rentals have helped part-time expats to minimize costs and, in some cases, make handsome profits!

HOUSE-SITTERS

As homeowners, you are on the flip side of those who are living rent free! You can access the same sites mentioned before in the *Living for Free* section as a homeowner seeking a house-sitter. A house-sitter is helpful for your piece of mind, and to keep your home from attracting thieves, squatters, and other problematic situations.

If you live along the coast or in the jungle, the humidity can literally rot parts of the house if it's left unused. Rust and mold may destroy your appliances, AC units, and the woodwork in your home.

TRAVEL INSURANCE

If you spend no more than 6 months in one location at a time then purchasing travel insurance may be the best option for you. For more information see the *Healthcare* section.

«THE MOVING BLUES»

"Accept that in the first few months you may be brought to tears by the most innocuous of things. This doesn't mean you are going mad or failing; it's just part of the journey of adjustment to massive change. Cry when you need to then be determined to make the best of the next day."

~ Johanna: Irish Nomad in Malaysia

There are aspects of Mexican culture that can take some time to grow accustomed to. If you are the kind of person that needs to follow a regimented routine to stay sane, check that attitude at the border. Unless you have a lot of money to throw around or friends in the right places, things probably won't get done at the drop of a hat. This laid back nature is one of Mexico's best qualities, but also something that has frustrated and will continue to frustrate expats until the next revolution. On the flip side, that's why you decided to come to Mexico in the first place! To Relax! You can start by accepting that the pace of life is just different here.

Aside from the lack of any sense of urgency, there are other bumps in the road that expats encounter adjusting to their new life. Whatever your annoyance, it's important to remember that it takes time to adjust to life in another country. Don't be to hard on yourself and get upset if you're not

blending in overnight. Be patient, take things as they come, and focus on learning something new everyday.

EXPAT EXPERIENCE

"The most difficult and frustrating aspect of life here is the same I find everywhere in Mexico-the traffic; not the lack of laws, but putting them into action. Also, the problems with water for so many people, and never finding a way to use the tremendous rainfalls to benefit the population....a long list....but just a mosquito in the total picture. We live in a time of change, and some are helpful, and others are taking us backwards. Again, adaptation is vital. Accept and find a way to adapt to what you cannot change; and spend some time giving back to what you can change."

~ Constance Baldwater, on the most difficult aspect of adjusting to life in Mexico

---

There are expats that have grown bitter and disgruntled. The most common cause is hyper-fixation on differences and change. They're like salmon, they flow along with all of the excitement and arrive to fertile international lands and the party is on! Shortly thereafter, they realize it is not what they thought it would be and flip a 180. They swim upstream fighting the way things are, and fighting the nature of the country that once attracted them. They're left exhausted and eventually caught, and served for dinner.

In order to have a healthy relationship, you must love your partner for exactly the person they are today with their faults, their gifts, and everything in-between. So too, you must appreciate your new country for exactly what it is today in order to live a healthy and happy life here.

I'm hopping off of my soap box now...

In every move I've made, I experienced a roller coaster of emotions. If you plan for it, it can take the edge off *a little*. Expect to have an initial high followed by an intense low. The low is mostly due to loneliness, culture shock which will be discussed next, and inaccurate expectations.

Change causes stress no matter what kind of stress it is. Moving to an amazing country that fits you perfectly is still a stressful event. There are concerns you will have and worries of endless logistics: shipping your car, container, luggage, pets, new house, new area, language acquisition, new foods, access to utilities, etc.

A key method for quick acclimation is to go out and make friends in the community. Find out the inner workings of the community and how you can contribute! If you spend all day interacting with those you left back home on Skype or magicJack then you've only left in body and are cheating your experience.

CULTURE SHOCK

This is not a phenomena that happens to the weak. It can slug you in the face or slowly tighten around you like a boa constrictor! Merriam - Webster describes culture shock as, "A sense of confusion and uncertainty sometimes with feelings of anxiety that may affect people exposed to an alien culture or environment without adequate preparation."

There are four stages of culture shock, much like grief.

» Honeymoon phase

» Negotiation phase

» Adjustment phase

» Mastery phase

♦ **Honeymoon Phase**

The honeymoon phase is the high I mentioned earlier. No wrong could be done to you or by you. You're romanticized by the differences in the culture, pace, way of life, and new exotic foods. Just like the honeymoon phase in a new relationship, you are blinded to any faults of your lover. Not until the dust settles does their obnoxious habits start to crawl under your skin, and you see the real them.

When your electricity goes out in a storm, or your water gets shut off for a day or two, or you are overcharged for a service and you can't get anyone to help fix it, those not-so-sexy parts of Mexico sneak up and bite you.

♦ **Negotiation Phase**

This is when reality settles in. When you sit down and wonder what have you done? All of the differences initially seen as romantic are all of the sudden cause for great concern. Can you really do this? Can you adjust to so many changes?

You realize how incredibly far away you are from "home" and your family. Maybe you don't know a soul in your new country. If you aren't fluent in the local language, that carries with it an invisible wall. While you can't see the wall, you feel it in every interaction. You feel it when you have trouble ordering meat at the butcher counter, or paying your water bill, finding the sugar in the supermarket, or asking the bus driver how much the fare is. Additionally, it can be hard to adjust to the tropical climate (beach goers) and new food.

This phase is not pleasant and those who successfully navigate through it are gentle and patient with themselves. They also laugh at their mistakes, learn from others, and resolve that they are no longer in a hurry and no longer in the US. They learn and adopt realistic expectations.

♦ **Adjustment Phase**

During this phase you have become accustomed to some of the new changes, like how long it takes to get your food while eating out and the long lines at the bank. You no longer fight the changes, you become accepting and build your routine around them. The changes become your new normal. Your understanding of the culture becomes more in-depth here, and you begin to cultivate connections with the community.

♦ **Mastery Phase**

You feel 100% comfortable in your new culture. You accept the practices and participate in many aspects of the culture. You may not completely lose your culture of origin, but you are now an expert in the way of your new country. You can navigate through any hurdle or problem as they arise knowing the appropriate course of action. You are ready to take a new expat under your wing and pass forward the experiences and knowledge that countless expats gave to you.

«BASIC PHRASES TO GET YOU STARTED»

Mexican Slang

Just like everywhere else in the world, Mexicans have an arsenal of slang dialect. Even if your Spanish is phenomenal, you'll find yourself struggling to keep up with your Mexican friends and their ever changing, often vulgar lexicon. I've provided a handful of phrases to get you started. To give you an idea of the loose meaning of some phrases, I've provided the literal translation versus the actual definition.

Keep in mind that Mexico is an enormous country and basic phrases and slang can be region specific. Just like Californians have different slang from those in Louisiana.

» **Echar la hueva**- to be lazy, hang around, chilling out Ex: Pase todo la fin de semana echando la hueva!
   I spent the whole weekend hanging around.

- » **La flojera**-laziness

- » **Ganas**- Desire
  Ex: No tengo las ganas de salir

- » I don't feel like going out

- » **Fresa**- Word commonly used to describe snobby people or establishments Ex: No me gusta esa lugar, el ambiente es demasiado fresa!- I don't like that place, the mood to too snobby!

- » **A ver que sale**- We'll see what happens

- » **Orale!**- Right on, hell yea

- » **Mala muerte**-a place of ill repute

- » **Guey**(prounounced wey)- dude

- » **Chilango**-A citizen of Mexico City

- » **Pinche**-damned

- » **Chido**-cool

- » **La banda**-group of friends, crew

- » **Cachonda**/o (a for female, o for male) -horny

- » **Neta?**- Really?!

- » **Chamba**-a job, often a lousy one
  *can also be used as a verb: El sabado tengo que chambear

- » **Que Pedo?** - Literal Translation: What's fart?
  What it actually means: Whats up?

- **Que Oso**!- Literal Translation: What Bear! What it actually means: How embarrassing!

- **Que onda?** Literal Translation: What Wave! What it actually means: What's going on?

- **No Mames!!** Literal Translation: Don't suck What it actually means: No F*&%$ way!

- **Estoy Crudo** Literal translation: I am raw What it actually means: I am hungover

- **Donde esta la peda?** Literal Translation: Where is the fart? What it actually means: Where is the party?

- **Ando bien pedo**- I am very drunk!

- **No hay pedo**- There's no problem

- **Aguas!** Literal Translation- Waters! What it really means- Be careful Ex: Aguas si andas en esa barrio por la noche Careful walking en that neighborhood at night

- **No Manches!** - Literal Translation: Don't stain What it actually means- Unbelievable!

- **A huevo!**- Literal Translation- To Egg! What it actually means- Hell yeah!

- **Que gacho**-How bad/unfortunate

- **Vete a la verga**- Go to hell!

- **Slang for $$$**- feria, plata, lana

- **Guacala**- gross!

- **Desmadre**- disaster

» **Chela**-beer

» **Chafa**-low quality

» **Naco**-lower-class, uncultured

» **Codo**-means elbow, but it is slang for cheap. No seas codo - Don't be cheap!

» **Chavo/Chava**-slang words for kids

» **Carnal**-close friend, close relative(literally flesh)

» **Tengo prisa**- I'm in a hurry.

» **Chingar**- Probably the most diverse vulgarity in the Mexican lexicon. There is literally an entire 200-page book dedicated to it's

» use called the *Chingonario*.[46] If you are going to be living in Mexico, it is a worthy investment. You'll be amazed that one word can have some many different meanings.

This list barely cracks the surface. For a more exhaustive compilation of Mexican slang, check out <u>Cabo Bob's Mexican slang 101</u>[47] book!

---

[46] available here: http://amzn.to/1vUr57q
[47] purchase: http://bit.ly/slangMx

NO BORDERS? Your Health Insurance Shouldn't Have Them Either. No Matter Where YOU Are, *We Have YOU Covered!*

"Insuring People All Over the Globe Since 1992"

- Premier Global Major Medical Cover
- Temporary Travel Medical Cover
- Life Insurances

Fast, Free Customized Quotes.... Contact us Today at john@expatglobalmedical.com or go to our website at www.expatglobalmedical.com

«PACKING TIPS»

♦ **Plates and Flat China**

Begin with the larger items. Smaller items can go toward the top. Wrap each piece individually with several pieces of newsprint. Next, wrap three to five previously wrapped plates together and stand each bundle on its edge. Never lay plates flat. Add 3-4 inches of crumpled paper and a cardboard divider before creating a second level.

♦ **Glassware and Crystal**

Always individually wrap each glass and never put one piece inside another. Place on the very top level of your carton and pack rim down. Especially fragile items should be packed in a separate carton and then packed in a larger carton surrounded by cushioning.

♦ **Bowls**

Wrap individually and then nest two to three together and wrap as an entire package. Place on end or flat. Use crumpled paper and a cardboard divider before adding layers.

♦ **Lamps**

Remove shade, bulb and harp assembly. Double wrap the bulb and harp assembly. Wrap the base and cushion it in a dish pack or similar type box. For lampshades, select the carton size close to the shade measurements. Pack only one shade per container. Don't use crumpled newsprint inside or around the outside of the shade. Glass lampshades and chandeliers should be professionally packed in sturdy crates.

♦ Food

Of course, never pack perishable items, aerosol kitchen products or frozen food. Box dry foods in medium-sized cartons after taping any openings or tops closed. Jars should be also taped shut and wrapped as well as cushioned. Pack cans and jars in smaller cartons.

♦ Clothing

Clothing can be left in sturdy dressers or packed in suitcases, if desired. Other foldable clothing should be packed in medium-sized cartons. Hanging clothing should be packed in wardrobe cartons. If wardrobe cartons are not used, be sure to remove hangers and pack in lined cartons. Hats should be left in their boxes and packed in moving cartons. Small boxes loosely filled with newsprint also help protect hats.

♦ Mirrors, Glass Table Tops, Pictures, Paintings, etc.

We recommend purchasing special boxes for all but the smallest items in this category. Mirror and picture cartons can handle most items. Only one article should be packed in each carton. You will want to consider professional crating assistance for oversized or heavy items such as table tops.

♦ Glasses and Cups

Wrap individually. Cups with handles should be cushioned with another layer of paper. Pack with rims down. Cushion and layer with crumpled paper.

♦ Books

Pack in smaller boxes with open edges alternating with the bindings. Hardcover books, or those with fragile covers should be wrapped for protection.

♦ Draperies and Curtains

Wardrobe cartons are excellent for hanging curtains and drapes. You can also fold them and pack in boxes that have been lined with clean newsprint.

♦ Bedding

Mattresses must be covered to protect them from soil and damage. Appropriate sized cartons are recommended.

◆ Small Appliances

Clocks, radios and other small appliances should be individually wrapped and packed along with linens and towels or surrounded with crushed paper for protection.

◆ Flowers and Plants

Artificial flower arrangements should be carefully wrapped and packed in individual cartons. If possible, secure the arrangement to the bottom of the box. Cushion and label appropriately.

◆ Electronics

Original manufacturers packaging with Styrofoam inserts provides the best protection for moving electronic goods. If these are not available, large or medium cartons should be used and the item well wrapped and cushioned. Larger home electronics such as consoles and large screen TVs should not be packed and will be moved as furniture. Computers and grandfather clocks require special pre-move preparation.

◆ Washing Machines

Washing machines should have all hoses disconnected and put into containers. If you place hoses in the tub or drum, be sure to wrap the metal couplings with cloth or paper to avoid damage to the tub's surface. Unplug the electric cord and tape to the back. Secure the washer drum.

◆ Refrigerators

Refrigerators should be emptied of all food. Shelves should be secured in place or detached and wrapped. The electric cord should be unplugged and taped to the back. If there is an icemaker, it should be disconnected from the water line and drained.

◆ Tools

Any power tools containing gasoline or oil should be drained before moving. Gas tanks can be cleaned with brake cleaner. Long handled tools can be bundled then wrapped. Hand tools should be wrapped and packed.

* Packing Tips Provided by Stephen Aron with IFE[48]

---

[48] http://bit.ly/IFEshipping

COMING SOON

Becoming a Nomad

Becoming an Expat: Brazil

visit:

www.Becominganexpat.com

- To see changes in-between editions
- For additional resources like our podcast!
- To read our blog
- To discover what we come up with next!

Proofreading

Lisa Bailey

Editor & CoAuthor

Shannon Enete

Photography

Cover photo: Katie O'Grady